Diary of a Wimpy Dad

DAVID DIEBOLD

Monument Media
Dublin, Ireland

ISBN: 978-1-9162531-3-1 (Paperback)
ISBN: 978-1-9162531-4-8 (eBook)
2 4 6 8 10 9 7 5 3 1

Cover design by Millie Baring: www.millustrations.co.uk
Typesetting by Monument Media Ltd.

Printed by Mullen Print, Dublin, Republic of Ireland.

This book has been typeset in Adobe Garamond, a digital interpretation of
the roman types of Claude Garamond (1480-1561) and the italic faces of
Robert Granjon (1513-1589). Since its release in 1989, Adobe Garamond
has become a typographic staple throughout the world.

First printing edition 2021.

Monument Media (Publishers) Ltd
18 Thomas Hand Street
Skerries, Co Dublin
K34 HH24

www.monumentmediapress.com

Praise for **David Diebold**'s writing:

'Write about what you know, they say. For the most part, it's good advice. It probably helps if you've lived a life as down right odd as Diebold's … but it's his skill as a writer that carries the day … Very entertaining'
—Pat Carty, HOT PRESS

'Diebold's unique style makes you happy, sad and hysterical in a short number of pages. This is the type of book that you'll be sad when you finish. Diebold's experienced career in writing, chiefly in his award-winning work for the print media, is evident throughout. A brilliant read'
—Amy Finnerty, RTE CULTURE

'If you think I'm going to say 'heartwarming', forget it. Diebold's stories read like dispatches from a street-smart disciple of chaos theory under deep cover. Diebold (if that's his real name) skillfully pens revelatory case notes that explore the often unconventional nature of family relationships. Life-affirming stuff from a renegade spirit'
—Eamon Carr, IRISH INDEPENDENT

'Penned with dazzling panache … A survivor's tale and a survival manual for anyone who's gotten mixed up with the sticky business of families'
—Damian Corless, AUTHOR

'Rarely has something made me laugh and cry as much'
—Tom Dunne, NEWSTALK

'Deeply emotive … surprises on every page'
—Sue Leonard, THE IRISH EXAMINER

More praise for **David Diebold**'s writing:

'Diebold writes with the craft of a poet and the gravitas of a seasoned comic. Each piece is composed with great tenderness, clarity and sincerity combined with a zinging wit. You will roar laughing one minute and weep quietly into your hankie the next, as he shares a humanity to which we can all relate'
—Sophie Grenham, JOURNALIST

'I always feel like I'm on a road trip with Diebold when I read his stories—he can turn something as mundane as making a sandwich into an epic, emotional journey. His writing goes from deliciously funny to deeply poignant, sometimes in the space of a single sentence. All of his stories evoke a powerful sense of place. A few sentences in, and I'm transported'
—Katie Byrne, IRISH INDEPENDENT

'The diary we wish we'd all kept. Every teenager should hide this from their parents. This rocks'
—Liz Ryan, AUTHOR, FRENCH LEAVE

'Wise, funny and profound vignettes of family life'
—Nick Kelly, BROADSHEET.IE

'One of the cleverest and funniest writers I know'
—Rowan Joffe, SCREENWRITER

For Molly

'Queen of Farts'
She was a good dog

Disclaimer

The events described here happened a few years ago. It's actually taken me this long to feel comfortable enough to put it all down in a book. Just to be on the safe side, I've been careful not to mention my wife Emily, or children Zachary, Jonathan, Sammy or Jessica, anywhere by name.

Oops...

Now I really *am* in trouble.

The Party Killer

—Nuts? I ask, holding up a pack and cocking an eyebrow.

We've driven miles to a supermarket for party supplies for the eldest son's eighteenth – which is all, well, all rather awkward as it happens.

I mean, I actually remember being eighteen, I'd confided to my wife earlier, screwing up my face as I emphasized the word 'remember' to show how inconceivable it seemed that one of our children should already have reached such a milestone. *Don't be silly*, she'd said. *Of course you don't*.

But I do. What I don't recall is getting older.

The eldest shrugs at the nuts. —Sure, he says.

I toss in two packs. —Onion rings? I inch the cart forward.

Thing is, we could spend all day perusing the snacks, but there's no avoiding the elephant in the middle of the aisle: the booze section yawning open ahead of us.

I catch my wife's eyes and steel myself, sucking in a

1

single deep breath between clenched teeth before seizing on what I feel is the most appropriate course of action for a father under such circumstances: I fling myself onto the cart, arms wide and shoot off in the other direction.

Sometime later, still throbbing a little where my wife may have thumped me, I find myself loading two small flat packs of beer into the boot.

—Perhaps, she tells the eldest, —we should just hold on to one of them until you actually need it.

—Sure, he shrugs again.

—Where will we be again? I ask.

—In the playroom, says my wife.

—The… play room? All night?

—Yes. All night.

I swing the last bag in. —How much did we pay for all of this again?

—A hundred and ninety something, says my wife.

I splutter involuntarily then mutter into the dashboard as I turn the key: —Seems like a lot of money for a party in our own house that we're not even invited to.

At eleven that night the house is bumping and heaving beyond the closed playroom door.

—It's good we're here, says my wife. —You know, just in case.

The sound of live music begins from where they've found the drum kit and my electric guitar.

—I'm going to the kitchen for beer, I say, springing up.

—Eh, she begins, but I'm already squeezing down the hall past eighteen year-olds taller than I am. They eye me up dubiously. I shuffle through the hubbub, nodding politely but I only seem to make people tense.

—Hello, mister birthday boy's dad, deadpans someone.

I pop my head in at the band and they promptly drop everything and apologize. It hits me. I am the party killer.

—You're back quick, chuckles my wife before sticking her bottom lip out —Did no one ask you to join them for a jam session then?

We listen as the party peters out then we emerge to clean up while the birthday boy walks the last of his buddies home. Room by room, we read the debris like crime scene pathologists.

—Someone had a coconut, I rue, sweeping up bits.

We examine gifts, like icebergs emerging from puddles of paper, some of them so grown up: an anthology of Oscar Wilde quotations, some not so: monkey-face slippers.

I'm emptying half-full cans of beer down the sink when I feel a twinge in my chest at how grown up the eldest of our four suddenly seems; and us, waiting in the wings, 'just in case', and there, looking back at me from the glass of the window just above the kitchen sink, there's me, still feeling young enough to want to join in the party, yet for the first time, feeling so genuinely old.

Eat Like A Human

—Someone pass the potatoes please.

The dish is passed down one side of the table like, I imagine, a church collection plate might.

—You know what we should get? says the younger middle teen, holding up a chunk of dinner on the end of his fork and examining it down the bridge of his nose. Of course, I haven't a clue, but it's not really a question when it comes from the second youngest of our four and purveyor of all that is contained in a lifetime's worth of Ripley's Believe It Or Not books.

—A suction tube that takes your socks off? I offer, —then fires them in a rocket propelled capsule directly into the laundry basket?

—No, says the younger middle one, but he cocks his head in a way that shows the idea is not unworthy of consideration.

—A head prop, so you can take your elbow off the table

and eat with both hands, guesses my wife using her chin to press an invisible button in the air that makes him sigh, roll his eyes and collapse his arm all at once.

—A trapdoor under your chair, the older middle teen lobs in.

—No, he says, depositing the contents of his fork onto a slice of bread and rolling it into a tube, —one of those conveyor belts you get in a Japanese restaurant. Then you'd never need to ask anybody to pass anything.

He smiles, cheeks full of food, revealing dimples.

—Can you just eat like a human please? I sigh, unfurling an arm towards the potatoes and clicking my fingers. It's actually our last meal together. The same younger middle one is taking all his dimples and ideas on a school trip in the morning. He's never been away without us before, let alone for a whole week.

—How will he get through it, I ask my wife later, —without breaking his teachers' minds?

—I hope they know what they're in for, she says somewhat longingly.

—The way he rolls his dinner up in a piece of bread, I say, pretending to look horrified. —And that noise he makes when he blows his nose into a tissue, like a dog that's been in the pepper.

—The elbows on the table, the lolling head, gasps my wife in mock panic before looking out the window and adding, almost to herself: —He's going to miss his birthday.

The next day, the departing teen fidgets on the front porch next to his packed bags. When I go to hug him goodbye I'm suddenly surprised at how bony he is for someone able to fit as much food in his mouth in one go.

—The world record... he had once begun to explain through a face full of cookies, and I wish I hadn't put my fingers in my ears for the end of it, as I now wave the car off through the rain.

—We'll have your birthday when you get back! I shout, suddenly remembering.

I go upstairs and check his room. The older middle one who he shares with, has already kicked the mess over to his brother's side and is now downstairs blissfully hogging the PlayStation.

At dinner, I forget and set the table for six.

—Maybe we should fling food all over the floor where he usually sits, offers the older middle one.

—It's what he would have wanted, says the eldest dryly.

The dog stares at the floor balefully under the missing boy's seat.

—Someone pass the potatoes, I say, rather half heartedly. But there's nothing but the sound of munching and a scraping of cutlery.

Daddy-Shape Dent

It's a day or so before my wife is to overnight out west for an awards ceremony, but she's already firing off short, ear-shattering bursts of instructions like a Gatling gun.

When all three of the boys retreat to the cover of the house's furthest crawl spaces, she resorts to mortar fire, barraging the ceiling with salvos:

—SOCKS... OFF... STAIRS... *NOW!*

Her sights turn to where I'm elbow deep in dishes, as though digging a foxhole in the suds, but she notices that I'm actually looking past her, mouth ajar, at the sudden spectacle of the youngest one, the girl, who is ten-years-old, and is tip-toeing by in a turquoise fedora, tiny purple halter top, and what looks like a pair of denim underpants over her black tights.

—Where... begins my wife as I say *Wha...?* But the girl is first with something coherent:

—Em, who's in charge when you're away?

—Daddy, sighs my wife, somewhat despondently.

The girl makes a little clenched fist and hisses the word *yessss!* before vanishing.

—What exactly is that supposed to mean? I say, faking bewilderment, secretly pleased.

—Evidently you let her do whatever she wants.

—That's not entirely true, I say in a small voice.

But we both know that it is.

Next day, all three boys emerge just long enough to see their mum off.

—Don't worry about a thing, I call after her. —It's just business as usual.

She lobs me a disbelieving look.

—Remember when we all went away, giggles the girl, and just you stayed, and when we got back, there was this huge daddy-shape dent in the sofa?

I make a shushing noise.

Once my wife has gone, I track down the girl again where, rather terrifyingly, she appears to be shopping online for high-heeled shoes.

—So, I say, shaking off the image, —what shall we…

She cuts me off with the news that she is due at a sleepover within minutes.

—You're what?

—It's on the calendar, she frowns.

With the youngest one on her way and what boys are here now glued to screens in various far-flung corners, I'm left with Molly, now moulting by the front door and wearing an anxious expression.

—Come on then, I say glancing longingly at the sofa, and we stagger to the nearby seashore where I let go of the

10

leash and she promptly sprints off to the only occupied public seating for miles, hunches into a quivering muscle-bound knot and proceeds to strain.

I catch up just as she's celebrating completion, back paws clawing clumps of earth into the air over a clearly horrified couple frozen in the act of eating sandwich rolls.

—Sorry.

I huff over to clear up, but they've already crumpled up their meals and are binning them. —Cheers, says one of them hoarsely.

We flee home where I rip the curtains shut then dive into the sofa and cringe under cushions, emerging only briefly to call the cyborgs down from their consoles for feeding, then wake up sometime after 2am and stiffly extract myself from a deep, daddy-shaped dent.

My wife returns the next day, looking curiously rested.

—Has anyone, she yells at the ceiling, hands on hips, —been outside this house once while I have been gone?

—Nope, I say, glaring at the dog. —Just… you know. Business as usual.

Stabbing Random Buttons

Half term seemed to last a lifetime but as the last lanky school uniform skulks out the door muttering something dark and accusatory to do with a missing locker key, the sudden silence is delicious. No arguments, no computer-generated machine gun fire rattling the windows, just a sort of warm, damp odor of freshly washed hair and slightly burned toast hanging in the air.

I survey the detritus of nine days of cabin fever as I finally get around to gathering up cemented stacks of mugs and chocolate wrappers from a playroom that smells like a pet shop.

—We should just get rid of the rug, I tell my wife as she collapses back in the door from dropping off the girl, and I motion with one free elbow to the room full of gaming controllers. —You know, spread wood shavings instead.

—You have the best ideas, she says, scrunching up her face in a way that makes me think, just for a second, as only a deluded fortysomething man can, that my wife might be coming on to me. But by the time we've finished clearing a path through the rest of the debris, morning is already sliding irrecoverably towards noon, meaning we've an hour or so before the two teens lope back in for lunch.

—Seems like ages, I grin, heaving an exaggerated sigh as I finally corner my wife in the kitchen, —since we've had the house to ourselves. I wiggle my eyebrows in a way I think might be suggestive but, guessing by her worried expression, is probably just creepy.

—Um, she says dubiously as the floor creaks upstairs and we both look at the ceiling and I realise I have completely forgotten about the eldest, who we've begun referring to rather less than affectionately as The Lodger.

—What, they get half term in college too?

Honeymoon over before it even begins, we get on with daytime life in a house with, well, what turns out to be three fulltime live-in grown-ups, which, we quickly find, is not without its challenges. It soon emerges, for instance, how lacking in housekeeping skills my wife and I are.

—We're out of milk, The Lodger sighs, shaking the dregs of a plastic bottle in the air. —And there's no food.

Our speech and grammar also fall pitifully short. We're quite accustomed to each other's verbal tics but for the eldest, they are a source of considerable irritation.

—What exactly are you trying to say, he'll sigh.

In the evening when the other three are dutifully dispatched to bed, my wife and I find ourselves on the sofa, wrestling with a cryptic combination of remote controls.

Finally, The Lodger comes into his own.

Just days in to his college recess, and my wife and I relinquish responsibility for all things technological and simply wait obediently for the eldest to come and make the shiny box with the moving pictures work. That's when he'll flop down beside us, and we're three sets of legs, joined at the hip, all jostling for space.

In what seems like no time, college life resumes in a week, which catches me off guard all over again.

I wait in the kitchen in vain for the sound of The Lodger creaking around at noon.

Missed dinners stack up under foil in the fridge.

In the evening the two of us sit staring at the stack of remote controls with utter bewilderment.

—When's Dad coming home? I joke and we giggle like children, stabbing random buttons until something works.

Yards of Hideous Cobwebs

I'd like to say Halloween crept up on us this year, and with our lot fast outgrowing it, promptly disappeared like a ghost in the night. Then perhaps I could wax nostalgic about our years of pumpkin carving kids that are no more, of standing guard at neighbours' gates as they filled their goodie bags; our decade and a half of crumpled masks and groaning tums; of raking up wrappers and nutshells from every corner, the detritus of another annual spookfest that's soon to litter every lawn. But it's not over for us yet.

The mid-term break has seen my wife and me, both working from home, wade through busy deadlines, meaning I never quite got around to doing all the fun Halloween things I feel that Dad should probably do for one of the last times it's likely to knock a gnarled little rubber hand on our front door, yet the house was well and truly 'Halloweened' this year by its one remaining devotee, the girl.

She took to it with feverish vigour too, seeming to want to wring every ounce from it all, as if she's had an inkling that this time next year, with all the newfound sophistication her impending teenagehood will likely bring, there may be other things more pressing than painting ghosts all over the sitting room window and the agonised wait for tonight's annual six o'clock flurry of sticky, grabbing hands.

Meanwhile, what this means for us is we'll probably be ducking under cotton wool cobwebs for at least another week. Christmas has twelve days then the decorations come down and the wretched, wilting tree, stripped of needles, is finally dragged off to the council skip. Our house has who knows how many days of Halloween before it's crammed back into its box and spirited away to the attic. In fact, it's been two weeks already as I jump for the umpteenth time at the styrofoam ghoul flapping on a string at the window in the front door, while I'm filling a bowl with some sort of fruit-jelly eyeballs.

—What's up? says my wife.

—'It' got me again. Shouldn't that thing be facing the other way, not in at us?

This makes the girl giggle.

It's all very well for them. My nerves are shredded after a week or so of this, for which I mostly blame a bumper bag of large, lifelike plastic spiders that were this year's addition to our hoard of horrors.

—Seriously. Whose idea were those again?

—Mummy's.

She chuckles into her fist.

—Hmm.

—Look, she says. —What's that?

—Gah! I jolt uncontrollably at the appalling thing that's been blu-tacked to the wall by the phone.

—You know, there are all sorts of things that I think are fine that you'd find as horrible as I think spiders are.

—Like what? She grins.

—Like… cleaning up after the dog on a walk?

She frowns.

—But that's not scary. That's just disgusting.

—Or mopping up sick after someone's had too much chocolate?

—I had a tummy bug.

—Right.

Clearly I am now entirely wrecking all the fun.

There's no way around it, really. The yards of hideous cobwebs and plastic spiders stuck all over the house are here to stay at least a week after tonight, then who knows? Perhaps the box they're packed away in then will become mysteriously lost.

—How many more years of Halloween do we have?

I check with the girl.

—I dunno, she says, clearly not quite understanding the question. —I love Halloween.

—Yes, you do.

It's not as if my wife and I haven't put the effort in for the guts of twenty years, since the eldest first staggered up to a front door in his little Mr Potato Head outfit. And in the intervening years we've probably been through enough fake blood to rival the wave of gore that crashes over the corridor of the Overlook Hotel in *The Shining*. But now our three boys, all teens and world-weary sighs, are content to spend another fright night in front of a film with their respective friends and, odds on, next year our little girl will finally find the whole Halloween thing just a little too childish and awkward to bother with too.

At this thought, and for the first time, I feel a little pang of regret as I look at the ghost she spent so much time painting on the inside of the front window and the pumpkin she so laboriously carved with the word 'boo' in its mouth.

—After you bag all your booty tonight, how long until we take all the cobwebs and spiders down?

—Umm. She seems to be weighing this up as she smooths a crease out of her costume with her hand. —We could probably take away some of the spiders, but maybe leave the window and the pumpkin for… like a week?

I smile at her. —I can live with that.

—And then, guess what?

She perks up, eyes wide, glowing with excitement.

—What?

—It'll be just six week to go 'til Christmas.

~~OCTOBER~~
~~NOVEMBER~~
DECEMBER
JANUARY
FEBRUARY
MARCH
APRIL
MAY
JUNE
JULY
AUGUST
SEPTEMBER
OCTOBER

The Grinch's Brain Is Dying

The Halloween pumpkin is still outside the front door when the youngest skips in from school and plops down in a chair, opens a tin of coloured pens and begins working on a Christmas card, humming something that could be to do with bells going *ring-ding ding-a-ding*.

—My homework, she chirps, smiling and looking up to where my jaw is hanging in horror.

Too soon, I want to croak, but instead I stagger over to the computer and find myself searching for 'Christmas countdown' which promptly brings up an unseasonably jolly page called 'xmasclock.com' on which the legend 'only 48 days, 3 hours, 32 minutes and 49 seconds to go' beams back at me. Make that 45 seconds... wait, 40. Every time I blink, it seems, the blasted thing has haemorrhaged another half a minute.

—Seriously, I mutter to no one in particular. —Is this thing counting down in double time?

—At a certain age, the youngest boy offers from nearby where he's not even looking, rummaging through schoolbooks, —the human brain has lost so many cells that you're only remembering a few minutes out of every hour. That's why time seems to go by faster. Your brain is dying.

—Rubbish, I tell him, but secretly betting a *Ripley's Believe It Or Not Annual* that he's right.

—What did he say? asks the middle boy.

—The brain, I stutter, —something about time, uh…

But I'm already looking balefully back at that blasted digital clock shedding numbers in front of me and realising, in fact, that even the seven weeks it's cheerfully reminding me we 'only' have to go, is not nearly enough. Santa has two mortgage payments to come out of his account before then and, being self employed, a whopping great PAYE bill—plus his credit card is maxed out.

—Plenty of time, I sing-song hoarsely through clenched teeth, clutching the table before closing the browser with a decisive click of the mouse. That's when, in a corner of the room, under a struggling cheese plant, I can't help suddenly noticing a tangled string of red electric cherry lights from last year lying in a heap.

—Honestly, I call to my wife as she passes, —I could swear I only just took those down.

—Actually, she says, coming to look, it was ME who took them down. YOU left them up until summer.

—Oh, I say, a little relieved.

—Don't forget, says my wife over her shoulder as she goes, —we have an invite to a Christmas launch at a store in the city tonight. First of the season.

I flinch. —The *season*, eh? So, should we take the train in… or the *sleigh*?

—Train, says my wife without skipping a beat, —unless Santa doesn't want a drink when we're there.

—No no no, I reckon he could probably use a drink alright, I say a little too quickly.

Seven weeks, I find myself grumbling in my head as we sort the family out for dinner and take off for the train station. *Seven* weeks. Every bloody year I *swear* I'll be better prepared the next—and every year the 'C' word sneaks up behind me with its red sleeve and white, fur trimmed glove and snatches the bank overdraft right out from under us. This year, I can't help noticing, it seems to be parading around in full view, first week of November— kicking Halloween aside as it lumbers towards us bellowing jollily.

—You okay? asks my wife as stations hurtle past now in the dark outside the train window.

—Just seems a bit early, I tell her, —for all this.

—Ah, Christmas is lovely, she says cheerfully.

—Mmm, I say, hoisting a smile. It *is* lovely. She's right. It's also expensive too.

Walking through bustling, night-time Dublin, we pass the windows of the Kilkenny Design Centre, which have been well and truly Yule-a-fied, and I surrender.

—Wow, I coo, —let's go in.

The whole shop, I find myself admitting, looks gobsmackingly good and I almost hate myself for getting that warm and tingly feeling as I prod a fake-snow dusted twig basket of wooden reindeer decorations.

—We could feed the whole family for the price of one of these, I say.

—You WISH, says my wife.

—Actually, you're right, I chuckle ruefully. These are, in fact, a bargain in comparison.

We plod on, pulling our collars up and taking a look up Grafton Street, but the big store windows there are papered over. Overhead, men on top of little mechanical lifts are wrestling with huge racks of bulbs.

—Looks like they've still quite a bit to do, I observe.

We arrive at the Avoca shop for our launch. There's a smell of mulled wine and friendly people are bringing around trays with salmon and brown bread. Glittering goodies are piled up the walls on every floor. Everything oozes Christmas and, I decide, giving in once and for all, it's irresistible.

—We'll come back in soon for a little bit of shopping, whispers my wife confidentially as I nab my first mince pie of the year from a passing plate, —the two of us, maybe Saturday. Get a head start on things, you know, while it's still early.

—It'll be fun, she adds and, overdraft be damned, she's right one more time. It will.

—Bring it on, I munch, reaching out as another mince pie goes by. —Just bring it on.

Midgets And Donkeys

Certain moments in life make you suddenly super aware of the here and now, alive in a sort of slow-motion *Matrix* millisecond and wondering, *How did I get here?*

This, I decide, is one of those moments, as I find myself tethered to a bucking donkey while a four-foot, blindfolded cross dresser comes perilously close to removing my teeth with a hockey stick being swung in a way that could only be considered homicidal.

A crowd of children nearby shriek and make as if to scatter in all directions as the deranged looking animal at the end of the rope I'm clutching does a crazy cartwheel.

—Whose idea was this again? I hear myself say then I wince as the midget with the pink wig does a full three-sixty and narrowly misses taking out our kitchen window.

As it happens, the cross dressing was the idea of the youngest, eleven years old today; the donkey piñata suspended by a rope from the spare bedroom window, my wife's. As children's birthday parties go, despite the imminent risk of damage and serious injury, this one is, I suspect, probably no more lively than most.

Hours earlier we'd been standing outside in the November gloom surveying our overgrown wreck of a garden.

—We can't allow children out here, I said, as impressed as I was horrified at the extent to which our dog had defiled the lawn.

—Well, we can't do the piñata indoors, said my wife, testing the handle of the broom with a series of dangerous swipes in the air, then discarding it in favor of a racquet, before finally settling on a hockey stick.

—These kids all have gum shields, right? I said, flinching as she made a final, unnecessary jab in my direction.

So we set about preparing the back garden. *A family project,* declared my wife, meaning she would do all the work while I offer helpful suggestions from a safe distance and the boys stand around amid piles of clippings from the overgrown hedge, hands in their pockets, mouths hanging open.

Some hours later, the last of the back yard apocalypse is only just being cleared away when our party girl appears with a huge fake moustache and a pillow up her jumper, looking disturbingly like a pregnant Mariachi.

The first guest arrives soon after, a little boy with flamboyant pink hair, and soon the dining room is milling with moustache-wearing girls and boys in wigs, whooping it up like some bizarre children's Fellini film.

I look at the time forlornly, with one fist filled with sweets, lodged deep inside a paper donkey's bottom.

I wonder quietly if life could possibly be more surreal.

That's when my wife shoos everyone out back and we whip the piñata around from what seems safely out of hockey stick reach and what ensues might be the most violent game of pin the tail on the donkey ever.

It seems like it might go on indefinitely too, until a quiet little Asian girl whose mother runs the local Chinese takeaway steps forward and with a single awe-inducing overhead slash cut, entirely decapitates the donkey, showering everyone with shattered toffees and lollipops.

It's carnage.

Hours after the last hyperactive guest leaves, we're still peeling toffees off the living room walls, ears ringing.

—That was probably our last children's party, says my wife, meaning next year our youngest will be twelve, which if our experience with her older siblings is anything to go by, will be farrr too old for 'kids' stuff'.

I know that this is what she means, but I give her my best shell-shocked expression, eyes wide, mouth open.

—Promise? I say.

Six Million Years Of Evolution

What's on your mind?

I suddenly realise I've been staring at the blinking cursor in the Facebook prompt box for at least ten minutes.

Nothing. Nothing is on my mind. It's an excruciating time of year, an in-between time, too late for Halloween, too early to start spending money on Christmas; too cold to be autumn, not quite cold enough to be properly winter—we can't see our breath in the air yet in the house, so can't quite bring ourselves to turn on the heating.

I rub my knuckles, warming them as I sit at the keyboard staring balefully at the cursor again—*What's on your mind?*—realising this time that my mouth is now hanging open and I'm drooling a little.

—Perhaps I'm depressed, I tell my wife as she passes.

—You're not depressed, she says, —you're just bored. There's a big difference.

She's right. It's just that I hate this time of year. It's one big tedious hump to slog over and the calendar months should actually go, *September, October, November... November. . . November, December.*

I click off Facebook, which is starting to remind me of a scrapbook of irritating people's annoying postcards, and I log on to Twitter instead, which is more like some vast crowded room of cocaine-addled mental patients, each having an enthusiastic conversation with a wall but all at the same time.

Compose new Tweet.

I try to think of some event, some sort of milestone with which to mark the passing days which all at once seem to blur into one great indistinguishable soup of broken-record sameness, but everyone in our house is likewise kind of treading water this week.

The eldest is only just back in college after his equivalent of mid-term break and so, even if we see him between rushing off first thing without his breakfast for the train each day and poking his head in the door on the few occasions he arrives home before we go to bed, there's little to report. I do, however, notice that he seems to be growing a bit of beard, on one of these rare, late-night check-ins around the doorframe.

—If that's for *Movember*, I tell him, —it's cheating. You can't just grow a beard and shave it into a moustache on the last day, you have to suffer the silly bit that makes you look like a seventies-era porn star all month, that's the whole point.

He looks at me like I'm an exhibit, then the head disappears and the door slams shut.

—I suspect it's nothing to do with Movember, observes my wife wryly. —Just sayin'.

—Bang goes that Tweet then, I tell her.

I fare little better with the rest of them.

—Someone please tell me something about their lives, I announce at the dinner table, which is minus the eldest, as usual. His two younger brothers and the little girl munch at me in silence.

—Why? says the middle boy finally.

—Sofa stickumpin fufbook, muffles the younger middle teen around a fork that seems to be lodged in his fringe.

—It is *not* so I can stick something up on Facebook, actually, I tell him defensively, then a little more quietly: —I was thinking more of Twitter.

—Oh, well then, deadpans the younger middle teen and hunches back over his dinner with a sigh.

—I have something, chirps the little girl, —ask me!

—Let me guess, is this about you getting your ears pierced last Saturday? This *was* in fact a milestone, but since my wife and I had each already been pestered about it every day for an age beforehand, it was all a little less (jazz hands): *Wow! Wonderful!* and more (wearily): *Well, thank heavens, finally*, at least for us.

—Nope, she says, very pleased with herself and sitting on her fingers lest she give something away.

—Intriguing, I tell the table before returning to her with a mock flourish. —Do tell, I say.

—Well, she says, barely able to contain herself, then taking one big breath with which to relay the entire tale, —I was in the sitting room with my friend Heather and we were playing Just Dance 3 on the Wii and mummy came in and she just started *talking*. Just *talking* while we were playing Just Dance 3!

We all look at her in silence, then at each other.

—*Talking*, she grins, shrugging and shaking her head at the evident madness of it all.

My wife looks at me and blinks.

—Well, I say. —It may be a challenge to capture all the comic nuance of that little gem in 140 characters or less.

Truth be told, she's cheered me up no end, as I realise nothing necessarily important has to happen every day, even every week. Life goes on. It gives you a giggle or it doesn't, evidently.

My wife comes in later to where I'm on the computer again, Facebook this time.

—So, she says, —did you come up with some revealing little nugget of experiential wisdom to share with your 'friends'?

—You're kidding, right? I say. —I've just spent half an hour trolling through other people's posts and clicking 'like' on videos of stupid people running into doors and dogs going down pool slides.

—It's what it's all for, really, she says.

—Six million years of evolution, I say.

—Shift out of the way, she says. —It's my turn.

Smells Like Victory

There is a strict routine to how we begin the day in our house. Essentially, my wife gets up and thunders around, using the sheer power of volume to pry children from various bedrooms and into clothes. It's like a scene from *Full Metal Jacket*. I, meanwhile, luxuriate in thirty six square feet of duvet, listening to the distant muffled thumps, the searches for bits of lost homework or hairbrushes; marveling, as if for the first time, how much nicer it is on my wife's side of the bed.

It's a thirty-minute drama, the same script playing out daily, just a different shoe missing, another boy hunting for keys; our hysterically barking dog keeping tempo with the chaos; until the whole house shudders with one last slam of the front door then the car putters off through the cold, with whoever is last to leave racing across the green to catch up, one arm in their jacket, bits of pens flying from a flapping satchel.

By this time, I'm blindly feeling my way downstairs to make coffee before ungluing my eyelids in front of the news. And when wife and dog finally return, I'll likely be found in my office, helpfully figuring out the chords to a Wilco song on the electric guitar.

In short, some people may be 'morning people'; my calling is elsewhere. It simply isn't my time in the family schedule to shine.

Today, however, I have a feeling there's change afoot, which is distinctly unsettling. It's not quite eight and I'm already overdue on what should by now be the still-warm, evacuated side of the bed, yet there appears to be a body in the way, which I duly give an encouraging shake.

—It's almost eight, I murmur.

—Well then, grumbles the covers, —you're late.

—I am? I say, genuinely confused for a moment.

—You're supposed to be shouting at everyone, comes the weary explanation. —And I'm supposed to be downstairs in my dressing gown with a cup of coffee watching a bit of Sky News.

It finally clicks, where all this is going. —You seem to think I have the easy bit, I mutter, mock-defensively.

—I actually *know* you have the easy bit, she says.

—Okay, I surrender, getting up. I only hope she knows what she's doing with this role change business. —You realise, I announce, —that you're messing around with the entire fabric of the space-time continuum.

—Mmm hmm, she says indulgently, and from my side of the bed, I notice.

Turns out, getting dressed at this unholy hour is not without its challenges. Life is, I quickly find, taking ages to locate a single pair of socks with no holes, then shuffling into a bathroom that's an inch deep in water.

In a word, dispiriting.

The boys are already downstairs, meandering from room to room like automatons, slowly picking up a trail of cast-offs from the night before draped over banisters or furniture, like debris from a series of small explosions.

The dog follows me around with a quizzical expression. The TV stays off. There's no time for coffee.

—I know, I tell the dog as I do battle with a sweatshirt, —this is all wrong.

The girl is perched on a kitchen stool, spooning dry cereal deep into the hood of an anorak that's zipped up over her head into a sort of furry periscope, making her look uncannily like a South Park character.

—Right, I croak blearily, trying to seem confident, already sounding beaten. —Your school snack…

—I usually just have crackers wrapped in foil, directs the hood, between spoonfuls.

I find yesterday's offering still intact in her lunchbox.

—Perhaps, I grumble as I butter a fresh lot, —we should just throw these ones straight out for the birds, cut out the middle man.

The hood munches at me in silence.

Before shooing everyone into the car, I pick up her schoolbag and it tries to pull me through the floor. A hasty investigation turns up an English dictionary the size of a breeze block, which makes me feel oddly proud, but I put it aside, under the dark and watchful gaze of The Hood.

We putter off, trailing one boy across the green, his jacket half on.

Later that day, the children's cousins arrive to stay, but my wife is called away to help a sick friend. This leaves me to look after everyone on my own, meaning six children at the dinner table. But now it's *my* time to shine.

I conjure up mounds of spicy Mexican food, and even our teen automatons seem to be almost jovial. We all watch movies together and go to bed leaving the lights on. I don't see my wife until next morning.

When I wake up she's already pottering around.

—You're… I'm not… I mumble through a tunnel in the covers.

—That's okay, she says. I think I prefer it this way. She pauses, pats the bed. —Your side just isn't as nice as I thought it would be.

—I think I know exactly what you mean, I tell her, stretching to take up every last bit of space.

She closes the bedroom door behind her and begins shouting for the kids to get up and the daily chorus begins all over again… shrieking, muffled thumps, hysterically barking dog…

Everything as it should be.

Thanks For Nothing

Every year, we stubbornly observe the American celebration of Thanksgiving.

—There's nothing religious about it, I explain to whoever will listen, strangers in the supermarket queue.

—I'm sure there is, taunts my wife.

—Nope. Pilgrims… Indians… I mutter, unsure of the details.

Our Thanksgiving generally presents two problems:

1) We prepare more food than we can possibly eat;

2) Some American dishes are a little weird, like sweet potatoes with melted marshmallows. But as no one is permitted to eat a proper meal for about five days beforehand, neither is particularly an obstacle.

This year, by the time we all sit down, we are beyond ravenous and I resemble a hollow-eyed madman. Ten hours creating a meal that would easily dwarf the average Christmas dinner-table spread have taken their toll.

I try not to think about the car I abandoned outside the wine shop earlier where it wouldn't start. My wife collected me in hers, my arms straining under Beaujolais, wild-eyed, bags of marshmallows dangling everywhere.

—Before we eat, everyone has to say what they're thankful for, announces my wife.

—But it's not a religious thing, I add through clenched teeth.

—Well, it can be, she grins.

—Nope, I grunt.

—Mmphty-grrmmph, offers the first teen through cheeks ballooning with food.

—Um, says the next.

—Uh, says the one beside him.

—Who, me? says the youngest.

In fairness, I can't think of anything either, off the top of my head. It's difficult when you're famished and the table is creaking with food. My wife gives up.

Thanks can wait, I think to myself.

We stuff ourselves.

Next day, my wife drops me to the wine shop in her car so I can jump start mine. I pull the lever under the steering wheel to unlock the hood of the car and the thing snaps off in my hand. All the cursing prompts my wife to leave me to it, departing on foot so I have to pay parking on two cars while I go to find something to fix the broken lever.

By the time I get back from the hardware with glue and a screwdriver, a dog has crapped right beside the driver's side door, so for 45 minutes I have to maneuver around the mess on cramped knees, sweating and blaspheming as I strain to tighten tiny screws deep under the dashboard.

Finally, something springs open so I can try the jump-start, but the engine just dies, so I surrender and call a mechanic, who says he'll be an hour. When he finally arrives, my lips are blue from the cold. He can't start it either.

—Have it towed to my garage, he says.

The tow truck is 90 minutes away, so I flee to a nearby pub for warmth.

—How did your Thanksgiving go? asks the owner.

—Broke down, called AA, they're sending a recovery vehicle, I tell him, teeth chattering.

—Yikes, he grins.

I reemerge to find the tow truck waiting, and a parking ticket on my wife's car.

—Try turning her over, says the guy.

I turn the key and the car makes a distressing dying noise,

—Sounds like a faulty key, he frowns.

I look at my keys and notice a bit of plastic missing.

He pauses, then reaches down to the edge of the dog poop and delicately plucks out a tiny microchip with his fingernails. —Lucky, he says. —A new one might've cost you a couple hundred.

I call my wife and we drive our two cars home.

Later, when we all sit down to leftovers, I realise I finally have something to say thanks for.

—You can all go ahead and eat, I say. —This may take me a while.

OCTOBER

NOVEMBER

DECEMBER

JANUARY

FEBRUARY

MARCH

APRIL

MAY

JUNE

JULY

AUGUST

SEPTEMBER

OCTOBER

Like A Paratrooper In Occupied France

We parents are put on earth to shame our children, yet strangely this reasoning doesn't wash. Like it's our fault we humiliate them at every turn, as if we're doing it on purpose. Fact is, we don't even need to try.

It's a cruel irony that just as we writhe with pleasure, basking in the light of their magnificence, they shrivel with disdain. You can see it clearly in the way they wince.

These things go through my head as we fly along in the car in the rain to where our eleven-year-old will shortly perform in her school's annual Christmas show, and I am under strict instructions—she might have even raised a finger in warning—not to embarrass her *this time*.

You don't know how lucky you are, is what I may have muttered to the fogged up windscreen as we barrel along. You see, I know what it's *really* like to be shown up.

I was fourteen, trying to fit in and late for school when my father, on his day off, offered me a lift. Weighing up the twin terrors of being dropped off in public versus the horror of missing registration, I accepted, and it would be years before I could even begin to forget what happened.

At that time, we owned an ancient, backfiring VW Beetle which my dad had painted bright orange with a bucket of gloss paint, drawing stripes on the bonnet with a black marker. In fact, so preoccupied now was I with legislating for every likely jibe about the bloody car, I failed to notice what my dad was wearing: little more than a flimsy dressing gown and slippers.

All might still have been okay were it not for two things. Firstly, due to a previous altercation with a gatepost, the passenger door could only be opened from the outside. Secondly, as we pulled up to where hundreds of milling teenagers now turned to take in the spectacle of the backfiring demolition-derby Beetle, dad got out and trotted around to wrestle with my door and it 'emerged' that he wasn't wearing a stitch under his knee-length robe, something made abundantly clear by a sudden gust.

To this day, the sound of a cheering crowd induces a mild panic attack.

Tonight, I'm sworn to behave, but as usual we're late, so I drop off our star and her mother first, ensuring a) their door works and b) I'm wearing clothes.

—I'll find a place to park, I croak.

As it happens, I end up having to pull into a ditch where, later than ever and beginning to sweat, I hop out, lock up and duly descend ankle deep into a pothole of filthy freezing rain, spraining myself in the process and soaking one foot through. —Is that all you've got? I growl at the heavens through gritted teeth as I limp, squelching up the path, and, if there were a god, this is where he might have said, *actually, no, there's more.*

Completely overestimating the weight of the church door, a giant Gothic thing perfectly balanced on well-oiled hinges by some depraved practical joker, I'm launched into the packed proceedings, hair plastered to my face, as the door ricochets with a sonic boom.

For a second, I'm sure the hundreds turned my way might break into a sarcastic cheer and my throat begins to close. But all eyes are quickly back, as I fumble vainly for the glasses I've left somewhere, to where a vague blur may indicate schoolchildren ready to perform.

Not wanting to miss a thing, I limp madly, one foot squelching, all the way to the front of the church where, incredibly, I find a single empty pew and dive into it.

Fumbling with my camcorder, I turn to squint for my wife and give her a thumbs up but can't make her out. It's then I realise the entire junior and senior infant classes are about to begin The Nativity a few feet away, meaning my daughter isn't on for ages. But now the entire assembly is hushed as a high-pitched voice starts shouting something about shepherds tending flocks and I realise I'm trapped.

It soon becomes clear why the pew, where I'm now crouched like a paratrooper in occupied France, is empty: it's where half the cast files off between scenes, clambering over the lap of the mad man with his drenched foot and his camcorder, whose daughter isn't even in this bit, politely avoiding eye contact until they all have to clamber back over him again.

By the time my daughter's finally on, my bladder is shrieking louder than my ankle and the rest of me is covered in tiny footprints. Her rendition of Silent Night is, of course, only sublime. I might even have wept but am now so entirely preoccupied with making a visible fuss of her so that people will know I'm not just some half-blind, muddy, hobbled freak who wandered in off the street to film their children.

—You were brilliant, I say hoarsely as we struggle through the exiting crowd to find my wife.

—I had to stop a few times, she giggles, —because you made me laugh.

—Really? I did? I say, incredulous, then with a sort of unapologetic smug self satisfaction: —I *did*, didn't I?

Pee-Pee Dance

Christmas, it's all a bit like that movie Groundhog Day where Bill Murray, stuck in the infuriatingly jolly, snowbound Pennsylvania town of Punxsutawney, seems doomed to repeat the same day forever, doing the same things with the same people to the same tinny festive tunes, over and over.

But as cheap, hokey and camp as it may be, I love every mangy, threadbare scrap of tinsel, every broken little festive bulb, with all my heart. Fact is, I have never grown out of Christmas.

At the very first hint of a tacky festive jingle, my wife has to try to drag me out of the loft where I'm already wrestling dog-eared boxes packed with festive tat out of the eaves, endless strings of bulbs that have spent most of twelve months conspiring to weave themselves into inextricable tangles.

From Santa snow globes to selection boxes and reams

of bright, crinkly wrapping paper—even at age 45, the excitement of it all is enough to make me involuntarily break into the pee-pee dance.

Sadly, the same cannot be said for the lankier of our lot, who are fast finding the whole affair quite the test of their teenage patience.

This strikes me as we lope back and forth along our town's main street on what is meant to be a pleasant family outing to choose the tree, but with our three teens towering over us now, all long hair, hunched shoulders and hands plunged deep into skinny jeans, we look more like a band that's been on the road too long, sticking out one last tour together before calling it a day.

Only our youngest skips ahead, in her own little world, singing something that could be 'Winter Wonderland' over and over to herself in a high, tuneless little voice, like a talking Christmas toy after you've pulled the string on its back a little too hard.

As it happens, there are three Christmas tree pitches in the vicinity, each zealously guarded by men wearing Santa hats and stamping their feet to keep out the cold as 'Fairytale of New York' crackles incessantly from a tiny radio stained with spray-on snow.

—It's the Pogues channel, I explain behind my hand when one of the boys is in earshot.

My wife's tactic for tree-buying, perfected after years of hideous embarrassment over all our arguing, is to hover at a safe distance until it looks as if we're close to a decision.

Choosing a tree is a bit like a family picnic where you can never find the 'perfect spot'. I want our tree to be just right but I'm pretty sure the boys, at this point, just want the whole exercise to be done with.

—What about this one? I say, too enthusiastically,

wrestling a rather spindly offering upright and realising too late how utterly awful it is. It's a crooked, mean little thing, the Gollum of Christmas trees. I pluck a few stray pieces of straw from one or two withered limbs like it will make a difference.

One band member examines me like a doctor fascinated by a uniquely troubled mental patient, another makes a noise with his mouth that so perfectly describes derision that my shoulders immediately sag. The tallest merely turns away and begins stabbing at his phone.

The girl, meanwhile, is off staring glassy-eyed at a rather eerie inflatable Santa, mirroring it as it sways a little, and I wonder for a moment whether the out-of-date cereal I dished up earlier may have had a similar effect to the bad rye I heard once made an entire French town descend into hallucinogenic hell.

—You've found one! announces my wife, arriving a little out of breath. —Well done. I love it. Let's go.

—Um, I say.

—Wait, I have an idea, says our middle boy dryly from somewhere behind a curtain of hair. —Why don't we get one that actually, like, has some branches?

—Yeah, that would be helpful, says another mop witheringly from behind his smartphone. —For, like, hanging decorations on and stuff?

The man is coming over now, clearly curious about why his trees are the subject of such unmerciful heckling at the hands of the Kings of Leon—and I can see a look of mounting horror on my wife's face when suddenly our daughter pipes up from under a fir that's not dissimilar to the one I've just dejectedly dropped. —How about this one? she chirrups.

—Perfect, my wife and I say at the same time.

Back in our living room, we all argue over how straight or high the tree is before sorting through a lifetime's worth of ornaments. Then, as usual, everyone drifts away, eventually losing interest in the fiddly chore of hanging baubles after about the thousandth one, until it's pretty much just my wife and I.

My Christmas spirit is starting to feel distinctly damp.

But then the band reappears from where, it turns out, they've been untangling lights—which they promptly arrange and plug in. My wife and I look at each other, faces lit in the cheap glow as we admire our Gollum tree in its full glory.

—It IS perfect, says the girl, breaking from humming a shrill version of *Rockin' Around the Christmas Tree* as her brothers tower around her.

—I don't know about perfect, I say to no-one in particular, —but it's not bad. It's not bad at all.

On All Fours, Hocking Like A Cat

My life is a litany of Christmas debacles, I think to myself forlornly as I sit propped in an armchair like some great bloated tortoise on its back, still surrounded by the shredded detritus of this year's festive trappings, half a turkey sandwich in one hand and a rather ragged paper hat sagging over one brow.

From the moment I first learned to walk, it seems I have been wreaking havoc on the jolly season, somehow finding successive new ways to lumber roughshod over proceedings in ever more creative and appalling ways.

The first time was probably at the tender of age of three when my family was still living in California and I got up early on Christmas morning before everyone else and opened all the presents under our tree, then sneaked over to our next door neighbors and opened all theirs too.

I woke up under a palm tree some time later, two fuming families standing over me, my face covered in chocolate, surrounded by the chewed up and expectorated remains of several hundred caramels and dressed in someone else's brand new cowboy outfit.

—It wasn't me, I said.

Things didn't get much better as an adult and on one of the very first Christmases with my future wife, I insisted she leave all the food and entertainment to me, but by the time I got to the supermarket on Christmas Eve, all that was left was a single, miserable processed turkey loaf and a Dustin Hoffman movie—which I might have got away with had that movie not been *Straw Dogs*. Am I the only person in the world who didn't know that it contains one of the most gratuitously violent home invasion scenes in film history? Evidently I am—and how we survived as a couple to ever have children is beyond me, a true Christmas miracle if ever there was one.

But it was as a husband and father that I really honed my skills as the *Bad Santa*.

Once, I thought it would be a hoot to buy my wife the joke gift of a pair of edible underpants, but then proceeded to get drunk while wrapping presents late on Christmas Eve and labeled the presents wrong.

The haunted look on the face of my nine-year-old son as he tore the wrapping off a strawberry thong will stay with me forever. I quickly retrieved it of course, offering some sort of bleary-eyed excuse as I stuffed it under the couch, where I immediately forgot all about it, until the dog was discovered later hunched over and gagging, a single red-licorice strap still dangling from its sticky pink maw.

Another time, while merrily in the throes of seasonal spirit, I lurched outside to nibble on the carrots we'd left for Rudolph so the kids would wake up and see he'd truly been, but then began choking on the mulch and as a curious neighbor came to their window they were greeted by the sight of me on all fours, retching like a cat with a hairball.

—This is not what it looks like, I tried to croak through tears as they whipped their curtains closed.

The culinary crimes I've committed against turkeys, meanwhile, are worthy of a Nuremberg trial. I have scorched, torched, smashed, melted, cremated and entirely liquidated the corpses of various festive fowl down the years, once so spectacularly miscalculating cooking time using a combination of roasting bag and fan assisted oven, that I delivered what can only be described as a giant glistening balloon to the table of upturned, expectant faces—which, when pierced with the carving knife, promptly deflated to reveal a sort of thick, turkey smoothie with just a few bones floating around ominously in it.

—Um, dark meat or white? I recall whimpering, as I fished around in the mixture forlornly with my fork.

This year, we've somehow managed to once again muddle through my mishaps. Yes, I tipped over a pot of water and shorted out something on the cooker that exploded with a pop and now it only works with a loud and irritating ticking sound.

Yes, I may have somehow insulted my wife by woefully misjudging the size of the knickers I bought for her and yes, strange though it may seem that they still allow me to make dinner at all, I probably served up a few rather mushy, mystery dishes that may or may not once have been some sort of vegetable.

But the dog hasn't been ill and the neighbours are still talking to us. We've even managed to eventually find a way to chuckle with each other before the teenagers loped off with their mates, leaving us to clear up the debris.

And so I dedicate this to all the husbands and fathers who this week will have overdone it or underdone it; who forgot something critical or made a terrible judgment call; who ended up having to order Chinese takeaway as something nameless smoldered outside the kitchen window; or who are still searching through the bin for a receipt for that gift they bought their other half, the one they couldn't have got more wrong.

Friends and fellow family-men all, just remember that whatever horrible thing you've done this year, there will always be another opportunity to do something that is so much worse, all of this will pale into insignificance.

'That Wasn't Creepy At All'

—Smell that, I tell our fourteen-year-old, the youngest boy, shoving a copy of *Zombie Apocalypse* under his nose.

—Ink, I rant. —Smell it while you can, because thanks to e-books, I say, making a sweeping gesture over the first floor of Chapters on Parnell Street where our lot are supposed to be choosing books to buy with tokens they got for Christmas, —all this, I gnash, —could someday be gone. Just like vinyl.

—What's vinyl? says the girl.

I look at her like an exhibit. —You realise, I mutter, —we're witnessing the death of culture.

—Can I get a DVD instead? she asks.

—No, you may not, I scold. —This is all part of a family New Year's resolution. Less screens. More books.

—I don't really see anything I want, mumbles our middle teen.

—Me neither, says his younger brother.

—This, I say, not meaning to sound like the irritated Comic Book Guy from The Simpsons but nailing it anyway, —is the best bookshop in the city. You have forty minutes. I will be in the cult section.

We meet at the checkout, the boys clutching zombie and horror anthologies which I duly inspect and cannot fault. The girl has a couple of Asterix books I've foisted on her after being amazed to learn she's never heard of them. And a DVD.

—Journey to the Centre of the Earth, she announces.

—Go on then, I relent. —At least it's Jules Verne.

—No, she says, squinting at the cover, —it's Brendan Fraser and Josh Hutcherson.

We meet my wife and cross the road for burgers.

—After this, I muffle through a stuffed mouth, —we start eating healthy for the New Year.

As we're leaving, I see a kid at the next table carefully sliding a record into its sleeve, which, I notice, is Joy Division's brilliant *Unknown Pleasures*.

I cannot contain myself. —Where do you get your vinyl? I ask.

—I shop around, he obliges. —Markets, mostly.

—Joy Division, I say, making a circle with my thumb and forefinger and tipping him a wink.

—Wow, mutters one of our teens as we hit the street, —that wasn't creepy at all.

—Yeah, says his brother sarcastically: —Hey man, I love vinyl. Why don't we go back to your place and listen to some records.

—Yeah, chimes in the other, —I might have some vinyl in the back of my weird van, wanna see?

—I hate you all, I sniff.

—What's vinyl? says the girl, skipping to catch up.

We head around to Waltons where the youngest boy is looking to buy an acoustic guitar with money he saved and, after I personally test three, we settle on a moderately-priced Epiphone.

—He's quite good, I tell the shop assistant's dreadlocks as he punches in the transaction. —We have another guy on piano and one doing drums, I add proudly.

—Cool, he says.

I feel a tug at my sleeve. —Do you have a euro? says the girl, pointing to a kazoo.

—Here, I sigh, digging in my pocket.

We trudge back across town to the car, the boys laden with booty, the girl lagging behind with my wife. —Come on, keep up, I say. It's been a good day. Everyone has scored things their dad approves of.

—Our daughter says we haven't been to any clothes shops, calls my wife.

—Urgh, I mutter over my shoulder. —Let's make it quick.

It's our last day at the cousins' before packing up to return to our own house after Christmas. —We're going on a walk first, I say when we get back, a suggestion met with unanimous groans. —Hey, I tell them. —We'll be doing plenty of walking soon. Part of our new regime for the New Year.

We end up hiking miles and the girl gets cold because she didn't wear enough over the new top she wanted to show off. —Can we get hot chocolate? she says as a café looms ahead.

—Maybe, I say, fumbling for the last of my change.

—Yay, she says, brightening.

The kids' hot chocolates clean me out when I go to pay. I hand them around and the girl's cup promptly explodes, showering the muddy ground outside with tiny marshmallows. —Oh, for God's sake, I grumble, as she looks forlornly at her stained top.

It's only as I'm dragging suitcases out to the car a while later that I notice her head hanging low. —What's wrong? I say, crouching down to see.

—It's just, she says, a single tear popping out and staying there, —things aren't really going right for me today. She looks tired and sad and terribly beautiful and in a single horrible rush of guilty clarity, I recall our shopping trip; the girl skipping along to keep up and falling behind, tugging my sleeve for attention or cheerfully trying to please me as I blustered around embarrassing everyone.

—Well, I tell her, —why don't we just get you home where I can do what dads are supposed to do and start making things go right again.

After the long drive, the boys scatter but the girl plonks herself on the couch between my wife and I, and we watch back-to-back episodes of *The Office* then order pizza.

—It's part of a new regime, mocks my wife.

—Yes, I say, curling an arm around the girl. —A family New Year's resolution: more TV, less exercise.

My wife thumps me, the girl giggles, and it's a sound better than any music that this aging, deluded anorak has heard, on vinyl or otherwise.

Even, dare I say it, Joy Division.

~~OCTOBER~~
~~NOVEMBER~~
~~DECEMBER~~
JANUARY
FEBRUARY
MARCH
APRIL
MAY
JUNE
JULY
AUGUST
SEPTEMBER
OCTOBER

One Of Us! One Of Us!

—Please, implores the eldest. —Can everyone just pretend to be normal for one night? His girlfriend is coming to dinner for the first time and he could be forgiven for being a little apprehensive, given this family's history of tableside behavior.

—I'm not sure I know what you mean, I mutter defensively, getting up from where I've just been crawling around the kitchen in my dressing gown talking to the dog in what I think is a pretty good impersonation of Bart's bespectacled buddy Milhouse from *The Simpsons*.

To be fair, I may have some idea. Dinnertime in our house, despite all good intentions, is routinely a test of patience and sanity for everyone concerned.

It begins with the ear-shattering clanging of a cast iron dinner bell on our kitchen wall, something we picked up at a market once—no doubt originally designed to call workers from across fields for feeding, in its current confines it's more apt to set off car alarms outside.

Three of our four then file in to set six places around the long table, so that once the many candles we always have are lit, it all looks a bit like the opening scene of some surreal dinner-party in a Luis Buñuel film, but with the cast of the Addams Family.

The girl will then tug a single pathetic morsel disinterestedly around her plate before dissecting it with the slow and deliberate suspicion of someone trying to pry open a coin purse with a pair of knitting needles for fear of a spider inside.

The youngest boy, who delights in horrifying us with his eating habits, will have the most space around him and the undivided attention of the dog as he finds some depraved new way to force as much into his cheeks as possible. And the second eldest, who now converses entirely in deep sighs, disgusted clicks of the tongue and the occasional monosyllable, will sit hunched over his helping, silently hidden in hair as his mother attempts an interrogation.

Last to arrive is the eldest, who requires several private calls before deigning to tear himself away from higher pursuits to join the proceedings which he will observe wearily from as far away from the table as possible with barely concealed disdain.

His dad, God help him, is possibly the worst of the lot. I tend to get terribly over-excited when it comes time to eat and will at the very least rock merrily in my seat, giggling and chirping between mouthfuls: Rainman on laughing gas. I've even been known to disappear beneath the table shrieking as if attacked by a shark, simply because I happen to think this is hilarious. Perhaps it's a blood-sugar thing.

So while we'll occasionally manage to muddle through mealtimes with a half-hearted stab at something resembling normality, at best it's like being at one big Mad Hatter's tea party; at worst, the circus-sideshow feast in cult movie *Freaks* where a primordial dwarf staggers across the tabletop towards a horrified guest while the assembled carnival acts chant, *One of us, one of us...*

In short, it's the sort of spectacle which could quite reasonably be considered dispiriting for an eighteen-year-old seeking to impress his girlfriend at a family dinner for the first time.

—Sorry? I say, shaking myself out of this disturbing reverie.

—Vegetarian, repeats our eldest. —She doesn't eat meat.

—Absolutely no problem, I tell him. —And hey. Best behavior. I promise.

He looks slightly past me, creases his lips and raises one eyebrow: a resigned, deadpan expression which, were we starring in our own wry parody of a fly-on-the-wall documentary about family life, would be directed straight to camera.

What does one cook for a vegetarian teenager, that everyone might enjoy—particularly a family which often seems to be eating six separate meals simultaneously? As it happens, we settle on Mexican—meaning that while I stagger around from cupboard to cupboard wringing my hands in crisis, our eldest son calmly suggests fajitas, with peppers, side dishes and sauces.

Fajitas are the great equalizers, as suitable for careful assembly by our food-suspicious youngest as for flinging into the vortex that is the gaping maw of our competitive eater, her next older brother, or to hide under the curtain of hair perched next to him.

When our guest arrives, candles are lit but we forego the

usual ritual of skull-fracturing bell. Our youngest giggles into her fists, rapt by the presence of another girl, and we gorge without fanfare or incident in a manner some might consider 'normal', for fajitas at least.

And when we finish mopping the sauces from our faces and torsos, I fetch a photo album filled with pictures of the eldest when he was small. After all, our instructions were merely to pretend to be normal. He never said anything about not embarrassing him.

He tolerates what turns into a sound roasting, from behind occasionally clenched fingers, with admirable patience, eventually prying his girlfriend away to walk her home before the nightly ritual of washing-up descends into the usual hysterical chaos of noisy recriminations.

Slipping into the quiet of the next room, my wife and I continue to pore over the album which we haven't opened in years. —Look, I say, gesturing to the serious youngster with his furrowed little brow. —He was always the only grown-up, even when he was five.

—I know, she says, slipping an arm through mine as the sound of something shattering in the next room is followed by a howl. —Where did we go so right?

Mouth Hanging Open

—Is this how it begins, I'm thinking to myself, —the long slide from middle age into senility?

—You must be getting quite used to these things, says the woman I vaguely think I should recognize but who will probably be offended to know I am drawing a blank.

We're sitting in a line at the parent teacher meetings for the youngest boy in his secondary school and I have a list of subjects to get through which I've divided up with my wife, who is off somewhere queuing for an English teacher while I'm stuck here waiting for maths.

—Um, I tell her, mouth gulping like a fish, but what I'm thinking is, *Deirdre? Dee? Debs? Deborah? Something beginning with D...* How do I explain that it's not my fault that my brain is obviously deteriorating by the second, that we're just lucky I'm not wearing nappies.

—Seems like only yesterday they were in primary school, she coos wistfully.

—God be with the days, I say and begin frantically fiddling with my phone. —Oops, better take this, I tell her, mouthing the word 'English' meaningfully, like it's a call from hospital.

I flee to the relative safety of nebulous corridors nearby. Now what? Perhaps I should put on my shades. There's a text on the phone: *Still waiting. Make sure you see history teacher. R7.*

R7? This whole expedition is starting to feel like a confusing episode of *Lost,* which is precisely what I am now as I find myself wandering aimlessly from corridor to corridor.

I'm soon rescued by a patrolling child, one seemingly assigned to round up wayward dads and frog march them through this warren to the next queue of flustered parents. She expertly plucks the list from my hand to see for herself where it is I'm supposed to be.

—Don't mind my notes, I tell her, squinting at all the spider webs I've drawn; the obscene figures, the game of noughts and crosses, —they're just for my... records.

She doesn't look up, just sets off, politely motioning for me to follow.

—I suppose you're quite accustomed to all this, I puff as she clips along ahead of me.

—Heh-heh, she titters politely, not looking around. Perhaps small talk with strange, unshaven, middle-aged men who wear sunglasses indoors is discouraged. I can't imagine why.

—Here, she says, stopping so abruptly that my feet skitter and I only just manage not to fall over her onto the floor taking her with me—a spectacle which, were it to happen, actually might, I suspect, be frowned upon.

—Oh, I say looking up, but what I mean is *ugh* as I'm

greeted with the sight of four more queues of pen-chewing parents, snaking away out of sight. —Perhaps I'll just forget this one for now, I say sheepishly, fumbling for the dog-eared list again. —Do you think you could just take me back to the, um, uh… But my helper has evaporated.

—Oh, hi! I hear with dismay. Another parent I don't recognise. —How are you getting on?

—Oh fine, just fine, I lie, taking a seat in line for a teacher who, I notice, doesn't look much older than our college-student eldest. I frown at my ragged list again like there's something important there before we're mercifully bumping along, each to the next chair like a party game, until I'm next.

I approach the table tentatively and take a seat, feeling not for the first time as if I'm seeing a fortune teller.

—Diebold, I say, like it's a password.

She peers over her glasses at some sort of vast and complex chart divided into countless boxes filled with tiny markings, spreading her hands over them like they're Tarot cards.

—Hmm, she says, blinking at the rows of ticks and numbers. —Mmm-hmm. Finally, she looks up. —Well, you've very little to worry about here, she says and I blink dumbly at her indecipherable notes. *Little to worry about where?* I wonder.

—I see great potential, she says and I stifle a smile, afraid lest she ask if there's something I'd like to share with the class. Instead, she gobsmacks me with, —Your son is a pleasure to teach.

I am aware that my mouth may be hanging open. I've hit gold. —Thank you, I tell her, meaning it, then grabbing her hand and shaking it far too enthusiastically and way too long. —Thank you very much!

—But— she adds behind me as I charge off into the maze to tell my wife, almost running her down, as it happens, around the next corner.

—How's it going? she asks, frowning at my crumpled piece of paper.

—Pleasure to teach, I announce with a grin. —Are we done here? I think we're done here.

We agree that we are and begin making our way back through to what I hope is the exit, at one point passing the youngster who rescued me earlier. —A pleasure to teach! I mouth as we go by, motioning to my tattered list with my eyebrows. She flashes a slightly worried look.

—You know we've about ten more years of this, says my wife, referring to the fact that the youngest has yet to even begin secondary school.

—No worries, I say, hurrying her past the still endless queue for maths and on towards the not-too-distant prospect now of a bottle of wine chilling in the refrigerator. —Only, next time, I add, —perhaps I should bring a really long ball of string.

—Huh? she says.

—Never mind, I tell her and we step out of the labyrinth and into the night.

Queen Of Farts

—Molly's a good dog, announces my wife indulgently, to no one in particular.

I examine the creature luxuriating in a basket in a corner of the kitchen, four paws in the air, legs akimbo, like the bizarre centrefold of a magazine for canine males: Molly, single, brown hair, eighteen inches tall, hobbies include 'walk', 'snack', 'ball', 'beach' and 'paw'…

—It's unseemly, Molly, I mutter affectionately. She wriggles on her back, then snorts, one lip peeling away from an upside-down muzzle and hanging mid-air revealing teeth worn from years building vast cairns of drool-drenched rocks, each painstakingly excavated from our nearby beach.

—What is she like? I say. Because, in truth, while words such as 'demented', even 'downright bonkers', are often more befitting our seventh family member; 'good' may well be stretching things considerably.

Molly regards me with one crazy, white-rimmed eyeball as I conjure up images of her belting over the dunes, merrily trailing streamers of phlegm, a sort of furry ballistic missile, as toddlers shriek and dive for cover. Or parading across someone's family picnic, head festooned with the reeking entrails of a dead seabird she's just wallowed in. Or the way she'll perch inside our front window for ages, murmuring impatiently to herself in dog-speak, until the postman finally arrives, then go so berserk that the glass ends up opaque from snot trails (some of them terrifyingly high). *Did the 'burglar' leave anything today?* one of the children will chuckle as Molly trots back into the kitchen, sneezing proudly.

—She's not good, I finally decide. —She's great. The very best of dogs. Ever.

There's a reason for all the attention. She's due at the vet for surgery this morning to have a lump removed from her front leg, an expedition which, given her exuberant demeanour, is something we've been putting off.

—She'll be as good as new by the time you're all home from school, my wife explains while we lavish her with farewells. As if on cue, Molly launches herself like a rocket down the hall and attacks the front window one last time as the letterbox clatters.

—Well, as good as she ever was, I snicker.

She's brought straight to the vet from the school drop-off. I stay to man the fort but, more than once, find myself pacing despondently like a relative waiting in the corridor of a hospital drama.

It hits me how much of a companion Molly really is. The house seems just an empty shell without our usually omnipresent furry family member skirting ahead to manoeuvre herself between us and any given door;

struggling to be let out, then turning around and barking to be let back in.

Each time I distract myself with some mundane household chore, I think I see her from the corner of my eye, but there's only an empty basket, an abandoned ball or squeaky toy, unbearable silence.

My wife is back within the hour carrying only a limp leash. —She seemed happy enough, she says. —They've scheduled her surgery for noon. We can collect her when she wakes up later.

We go for our morning stroll along the beach, the two of us alone, but our heart isn't in it. There barely seems any point. Both of us catch ourselves continuously looking around for a zigzagging blur of fur.

Everyone is waiting by the time Molly wobbles back into the kitchen, still groggy, a row of neat stitches on her foreleg and a huge plastic cone on her head like the hapless hairy hero in the Disney movie *Up*.

—Oh no, notices the middle teen. —Not the Cone of Shame!

—It's to stop her chewing her stitches, I explain as the dog bashes it on a door frame then miserably drags a chair out from under the table after becoming snagged on it.

—I think it's going to be a long two weeks, rues the girl, giving the dog a gentle squeeze.

—She looks like the queen from Alice in Wonderland, notes our eldest.

Molly gazes up balefully from inside her funnel, like a big furry Flake bar lodged in a giant plastic ice-cream cone, then gives her tail a brief, encouraging shake.

—She's Shakespeare, observes her youngest brother.

—She's Elizabethan, coos the girl.

—She's the Queen of Farts, says my wife.

In fact, we all quickly become quite used to the dog's great, cumbersome, conical plastic cranium. Molly finds it has its uses too: as a floor scoop, like a Hoover attachment, for wayward kitchen scraps; and as a bullhorn to amplify the explosive spasms of rage whenever her favourite 'burglar' comes calling.

By the time the stitches are due to be taken out, she seems quite adept at getting around with the thing, though by then, it's so bashed up, it's little more than a filthy, ragged ruffle.

—Somehow, I don't think they'll be able to recycle it, says my wife arriving home with Molly in tow.

The dog turns to look then winces as her bare nose bashes off a book shelf.

—She may have to get used to not having a protective helmet anymore, says one of the boys.

—Poor Molly, says the little girl, giving her a hug, but then the doorbell rings and a furry missile launches itself from her arms.

Jangling The Change

—Wonderful, I mutter glumly as I consider the dark clouds jostling to hurl heaping handfuls of filthy rain at our kitchen window.

—I can't find a hairbrush, says the little girl balefully from the hall where she's staring at her hands. I go and pick one up from the glass table two feet away.

—Has anyone seen my locker key, sighs the second eldest, prodding a pile of coats in a heap on the floor with his foot. —Have you checked your trouser pocket? I offer, a suggestion met with a deep sigh before a brief, dejected search reveals said key in said pocket.

—I need three euro, announces his younger brother between messy spoonfuls of cereal through a curtain of hair. —Look under the cushions in the television room, I tell him.

It's just another dark, winter's school morning, only it's not. Normally, I would look forward to the silence after the last slam of the door, sighing with relief into my second cup of coffee while my wife does the school run and I settle into the quiet routine of working from home. But today I've a train to catch, a dispiriting prospect on such a gloomy day.

—Say hello to your dad from us, says my wife, delivering me in the car to the depressing queue of soaked raincoats at the station.

I'm on the platform before I realise I've forgotten my phone, which makes the journey south seems endless and very lonely. The countryside peels away outside fogged windows until the train is trundling between high walls plastered with graffiti.

There's little I recognise about the small suburban town where I grew up when I eventually get there. The shops I knew are gone. I can't even find a ghost of the child I once was, or the friends I knew, or the years I blithely squandered, heaving heavy schoolbags up and down the hill as I wished it all away.

Dad's wife answers the door. —You're right on time, she says. —Go ahead, he's waiting for you.

I find him ensconced in the corner of a leather sofa and I look at the oxygen tank, his fingerless gloves, thin legs that I remember latching onto while lying on the floor as a kid when his calves were still muscular from mountain walks, then he'd heave me around and bellow with laughter.

—How are you? I manage.

—Heh, he wheezes, meaning *how do you think?* But what he says between short mechanical jets of air from a tube is, —Oh, just hangin' in there, and I make a thin line with my lips in the shape of a smile and we regard each other with glittering eyes.

I produce the handheld voice recorder from my coat

pocket like a magician performing a trick, press the button and place it on the little coffee table between us and we resume a weekly conversation we've been having and slip easily back through the decades to World War Two, saxophones and Swing bands.

It's the larger-than-life story of a man from an era I never knew, before he was simply 'Dad' – and, over the course of an hour, I revel in the anecdotes, highlight of which today is the time he played a gig with Louis Armstrong and walked in on the legend backstage to find him sitting in his underpants, smoking a joint. Chuckling as the digital recorder counts down far too quickly towards zero, it's easy to forget why we're here: to collect these stories to share after he's gone.

When he shuffles off for a bathroom break, I look at the empty hollow he's left in the leather and for a moment I'm overcome with the urge to put my hand there and touch the warmth.

—You must have your own memories of him, when you were a child, says Sally, poking her head in the door.

I do, but where do they fit into all this? The feel of his bristles on my young face and the strong smell of his coffee and aftershave; the sting of English mustard in the freezing sandwiches we'd munch contentedly together beneath a tree halfway up a hill on one of the long hikes I would sullenly outgrow; the reassuring sound of him clearing his throat from behind his newspaper every night or his habit of standing noisily jangling the change in his pocket as I sprawled on the carpet trying to watch telly.

When he comes back in, it takes him ages to get his breath. —He's probably had enough for today, says Sally, gently helping him with a tangle of tubes as I nod my head uselessly.

Walking back to the train, the tickle of his whiskers still on my face from our goodbye kiss, I can't help wondering, will my children ever be interested in asking me who I was before I was 'Dad'? What will they remember? What have I ever done that's worth committing to a voice recorder?

When I finally fall in the front door, brushing off the cold, there's a pile of schoolbags and coats in the middle of the hall. —Is someone going to pick these up? I say, stepping over them into the warmth.

The little girl is watching TV and I stand beside her and jangle the change in my pocket noisily.

—What are you doing? she frowns.

—How about a hug for your daddy? I say.

—Urgh, she says without looking up, but I think I detect smile.

~~OCTOBER~~
~~NOVEMBER~~
~~DECEMBER~~
~~JANUARY~~
FEBRUARY
MARCH
APRIL
MAY
JUNE
JULY
AUGUST
SEPTEMBER
OCTOBER

A Fist In The Face

—Finlay's coming today, says my wife over breakfast, in a tone usually reserved for reminding the children to be on their best behavior. Only she's not actually talking to them. She's talking to me.

—Oh, I say, matter-of-factly, noticing the dog already hiding under the table. Two things are guaranteed to send the dog scuttling for cover: the sight of the apron we use when she gets a bath, and the name that heralds a day-long stay from our favourite five-year-old.

—Don't be such a coward, I tell the quivering puddle of fur beneath my feet as she heaves her head forlornly onto her paws and emits a deep, nasal sigh.

—Please, says my wife, —try not to get him too over-excited this time.

—I don't know what you mean, I say, mock-defensively. Of course, I *do* know. Babysitting our best friends' little boy is a highlight of any given week and I take no greater pleasure than winding him up like a top and returning him later a wide-eyed, cackling loon. We dads make the very best of babysitters. Sadly, it seems the days are gone when I can sneak up behind any of our own three boys, hoist one overhead and yell *how many times have I told you about crawling on the ceiling?* until he's breathless from laughing and begging to released. They've each long since grown too tall and too strong. Though I'll still get the urge to play, at the first sign of me approaching with a mischievous glint, they'll simply swat me away and glower *go away.*

My magic also seems to have worn off on our not-so-little-anymore girl, since my favourite game of collapsing halfway up the stairs and pretending to be unconscious seems to have finally worn thin. She merely steps gingerly over my twitching body, as though I'm not even there.

—Haven't you heard about the dad who cried wolf?

I'm sitting in an armchair watching the last few morning headlines when Finlay arrives and I look up to see all three feet of him standing inches away, grinning at me darkly, eyes blazing. Dennis the Menace.

—Weird, he announces.

—Hello.

—You're weird, he says. *Weirdo!* and I narrowly avoid him punching me in the face.

—Can you not do that? I tell him in what I think is a not-unreasonable voice.

—Poo, he replies and shudders with a full-body giggle.

—Look, I tell him. —I don't know who you think I am, but if you're looking for Dave, I locked him under the stairs a week ago. I roll my eyes white.

—Liar, he says.

I secretly tuck the wilted skins of a remaining half-banana from breakfast into my sleeve. —Hey, I tell him. —I slammed my hand in the door earlier and I think I really hurt myself. Look… I wiggle the limp brown fronds at the end of my arm in the air.

—Graaaggghhh! he shrieks and tears off up the stairs, sending something crashing.

The dog peeks around from the safety of the double doors nearby and promptly vanishes.

—Game on, I tell the empty room.

I revel in the role of torturer-in-chief for the rest of the day as Finlay whirls from room to room like a deranged dervish. It's a wonderful chaos that we too easily forget between these visits in the otherwise quiet normality of often sullen, computer-addicted teenagers. But Finlay brings out the children in all of us again.

When our daughter gets in from school, she exclaims *Finlay!* and drags out bins of forgotten dolls from under her bed, which they proceed to dismember together.

And Finlay is the one thing guaranteed to brighten our gloomy teens, whose elusive smiles will emerge instantly from behind their curtains of hair when they lumber in the door to the screams and disarray.

Before long, they're all taking turns thundering from room to room on all fours at Finlay height, cheerfully being clobbered with whatever's near to his chubby little hands to howls of *Get away!*

I try to remember them all at that age—the crazy five-year-olds so full of life that each of them took turns at being for such a short time, all just photos now in silent family albums stacked on shelves.

Something clatters to the floor somewhere and the dog lopes down the hall wearing what appears to be my dressing gown tied around its neck like a cloak. I catch my wife's eye in the kitchen where she lobs me a look that says, *This is all your fault, you know,* and we both can't help but stifle smiles.

When it's time for him to go, Finlay has to be pried off a table leg. —No, he laments. I don't want to!

I've already collapsed back into the armchair when he comes to say goodbye and I look to find him directly beside me, at head height, rosy-cheeked and disheveled.

—I hate you, he giggles and I receive a blow from a fist in the face.

We watch him being carried out, writhing and kicking, before being loaded in and driven off with a beep, then the house suddenly seems terribly quiet.

—So, how was school today? I venture to one of the boys, already nestled in front of his PlayStation.

—Eh, whatever, he says, so I launch myself across the floor and tickle him until he begs for mercy.

I'd kind of forgotten, I decide, just how good I am at that.

Almost, Not Actual

We're creatures of extremes, we middle-aged men, is what I decide as I scrub my hair dry and examine the sky outside our bedroom window, wincing a little at some nagging pain in my back.

Who am I fooling? We're just big kids, only achier. Even something as unpredictable, as uncontrollable as the weather, for instance, can seem to conspire along with the entire world to make this our 'best birthday ever' or 'the worst of all time'. But I'm still on the fence about which way it's all going this year when my wife decides pleasantly that we're to celebrate a day early, with an overnight stay in a city hotel.

—It's cheaper tonight, she reasons, —and easier to get the girl taken care of after school today… she says, ticking off fingers on the invisible clipboard that her hand has become for an instant.

I try to sneak a peek over her shoulder as if I might see

77

a nice surprise lined up there, or any mention of my name at all—but she conceals her hand tight against her chest as if there's really something there.

—We can have dinner somewhere nice, she continues, —and I can do my diet tomorrow instead.

—On my actual birthday? I sulk.

—*This* is your birthday, she explains as though for the umpteenth time. —Go pack.

I'm not completely convinced, but there's a wheelie-bag on the bed, I notice, one that appears to be already near capacity with several pairs of women's shoes, a number of her outfits, along with knots of knickers and tights.

—How long are we going for again? I mutter.

—Take another bag if you like, she says, rushing in and back out of the room again, organising things.

—No, I say, nose in the air, to no one. —This is fine.

I roll up a single pair of socks inside a single pair of boxers and deposit these in a side pocket proudly, marvelling at my own efficiency. —Done, I say.

We decide to drive the car in, which makes it feel even more like being on the lam.

—Only suckers are taking the train today, I say out loud as we sit for over an hour in traffic and it begins to spit sleet.

It's early afternoon when we finally pull in to the car park behind the hotel, so we check in and hit the nearby National Art Gallery, which all feels very *Ferris Bueller's Day Off* I think, and I begin to hum *Danke Schoen* like the lead character in what's actually my favourite movie. Of course, I realise, catching sight of my reflection, at this age I'm less Matthew Broderick, more Bill Murray.

We lose ourselves like this, meandering together through

rooms full of familiar paintings and statues, though the whole place seems smaller than I remember. We visit a painting of a little boy that we've always liked, but it turns out to be called *The Cottage Girl*.

—Who knew? I shrug.

And we finally find our favourite statue, a female form hugging a blanket to herself in a howling wind. This, says the little sign next to it, is actually a boy.

—They've changed everything, I say.

We seek solace in a nearby gastro-pub and munch in silence as we watch busy people struggling by in the worsening weather.

—This is the best almost-birthday ever, I deadpan, flagging down the waiter for second pints.

We're a little woozy by the time we agree to split up for an hour to shop, meaning she'll look at clothes and I'll walk around a few record stores and rue the demise of all that used to be cool; things we each like to do but hate being there as the other does them.

—Room service, I say, knocking when I get back to the hotel room again later. —I didn't order anything, says my wife as I let myself in, but I can see she's bought fizzy wine somewhere and found some plastic cups, which all seems to suit the almost-occasion perfectly.

—I wonder how the kids are getting on, she says, phoning to check as I wrestle with a TV remote control attached to the bedside table by a curly wire and *Come Dine With Me* appears overhead.

When we wake up several hours later, it's ten o'clock.

—How the hell did that happen? I say.

We narrowly make it to the first reasonable restaurant we

can find before the kitchen closes, settling for something quick just before catching the closing lines of a stand-up comedy show around the corner, the final encore of a band somewhere else, then hurried last orders at a pub.

—Happy *actual* birthday, says my wife, looking at her watch on our way back. —That was fun.

—You're telling me, I say. —Most couples our age would probably just fall asleep watching telly.

I twist away just in time as she goes to thump me.

—Ow.

—I didn't even get you.

—I know, I groan. —I think I just did my back in.

Tales From The Fridge

Every year we are visited with some sort of horrifically expensive mechanical failure. Last year it was the car, the year before it was the dishwasher. It's as though they wait for the most inconvenient moment, just as the reserve tank of your bank balance is coasting on empty, to give one last gurgle and go belly up. This year we've been in a month-long denial over the excruciatingly slow death of our fridge. It started with a chunk of ice in a little drain in the back. There was a plastic tab poking out which seemed to want pulling to clear the ice, which I tried, then staggered backwards as it snapped off in my hand.

I read the little embossed letters on the bit in my hand. 'Do not pull'.

An ice cap began growing from the hole, becoming a vertical glacier that froze anything near it on the upper shelves, but melted continuously at the bottom, engulfing jars and dissolving labels so that the various residues of ancient refrigerator sauces became dangerous enigmas.

—What's this one? says my wife one day, opening one of them, sniffing at it and wincing.

—Brandy butter, I say, squinting. —Never goes off.

—We can't keep butter from last Christmas, says the eldest, curling a lip in disgust.

—It has sentimental value, I tell him.

—It has fur, says my wife.

I look at it. —That's not brandy butter, it's Tartar sauce.

She rids the fridge of more mysteries: half-full vitamin bottles that no longer rattle; suspicious preserves, like horror-movie hospital laboratory specimens, and some sort of mummified chunk, unidentifiable through layers of clingfilm, that we're all too scared to look at too closely.

When the purge is over, she begins chipping at the ice cap with a wooden spoon and bailing out water, until the inside is pristine, almost new.

—That should do it, I tell her, nodding.

But within hours, the puddle is back. Within a day, it's overflowing into the freezer below. We bail and bail to no avail, until one day I wrestle open the freezer to reveal great filthy icicles encrusted there. It looks like a fridge from the Upside Down in 'Stranger Things'. I expect to peer into its depths and see the Demogorgan. I wonder if the flickering doorlight is trying to communicate something to us.

One day, I go to get some milk and a cloud of tiny black flies emerge. The milk has turned into butter overnight and yogurts into watery cheese.

—I think it's actually started heating things.

Still we refuse to give up on the wretched thing. We try a de-frost and the freezer discharges most of its weird post-apocalyptic winter cave into dirty piles of dish towels and then we go to start it back up.

I pause for effect. —Clear! I yell and slap the plug back in. Nothing. I give the fridge a firm shake. —Come on! Not today you don't. Stay with me!

It rattles and gasps and within hours the freezer resumes its slow trudge towards Antarctica, but up above, temperatures remains balmy, and when the eldest comes home, I tell him his dinner is warming in the fridge, next to the two-litre bottle of cottage cheese.

—Think I'll pass, he says.

We resort to freezing plastic bottles of water and ferrying them in to the fridge to keep whatever is still edible from growing a fur coat.

—I'm afraid she's had it, I finally tell my wife. —I'm going to call this. I glance at the clock. —Fourteen after seven.

I unplug the fridge. It doesn't even gasp.

We call the repair man.

—The only thing we could see was a red light in a panel next to the word 'compressor', we tell him.

—Hmm, he says. —Could be a compressor problem.

—You reckon?

—How old was it?

I note the emphasis on the word 'was' and my heart sinks a little. We bought the fridge the same year we got the dog. I put my hand over the phone.

—How old is the dog? I hiss at my wife.

—Fourteen, she says.

—Thirteen and a half, I tell him.

—Honestly? he says. —Maybe it's time you shopped around for a new fridge.

It feels like a betrayal to peruse prices on the internet while our old fridge is still barely cold. The cheapest we find is about €350.

The youngest boy pipes up.

—Whose birthday is it next?

It's the middle boy's, in mid-March, as it happens.

—I'm sure he could do with a new fridge, he says.

—And hey, if it won't fit in his room, we could always…

—You, says my wife, —are a genius.

I look over to where she's wrestling the smouldering toaster for a defrosted waffle.

—And whose birthday is after that? I grin.

OCTOBER
NOVEMBER
DECEMBER
JANUARY
FEBRUARY
MARCH
APRIL
MAY
JUNE
JULY
AUGUST
SEPTEMBER
OCTOBER

Sugar And Slobber

—Nothing to see here, announces the girl at the top of her voice, shaking her coat off one arm, flinging it into the middle of the hall floor and parading over it into the kitchen, drooling dog in tow, and placing a large, rather battered biscuit tin proudly on the table.

—I said, *nothing to see here*, she yells if no-one has come yet, though usually they're on the way by now, because the whole family knows what this phrase means. Originally just a cue for my wife and I to come and coo at the results of her weekly afterschool cookery class: rock buns, scones, brownies and shapeless cakes of all description, all crammed into a warm rectangle shape, now it has become quite the anticipated event.

So there'll be a thunder of hooves from every corner of the house as her brothers jostle for their share of this week's creation, painstakingly measured by our diminutive host and divided into six, precisely even pieces.

85

If someone is missing from the line-up, their portion is placed carefully into the centre of a piece of notepaper on which is inscribed scrupulous instructions relating to who it is for, who is not allowed to touch it and how it is to be consumed: *Eat warm* or *Have with glass of milk*.

And heaven help anyone who isn't hungry, they'll be relentlessly followed from room to room with their helping until it is consumed to the satisfaction of the face peeking around the doorframe.

—At least she doesn't do that thing anymore, I confide to my wife, —you know, the force feeding.

—Urgh, she replies, scrunching her nose and shaking her head as if trying to rid herself of the memory.

Because there was a time, in our daughter's toddler days, when a refusal to accept the offer of some sweet, thoughtfully pre-chewed treat, resulted in it being stuffed into your mouth by a sticky little hand, usually when you least expected it, while reading a magazine or while on the phone to someone.

The sentiment has changed little, but thankfully she has since graduated to more complex kitchen creations than neon modelling clay coated in sugar and slobber; to actual baked goods, many of which are accompanied by helpful notes with suggestions such as *Eat this*.

In short, if the girl ever becomes a chef (and any momentary mental image of Kathy Bates hand-feeding James Caan in *Misery* is almost entirely unjustified) pity the punter who sends back a plate with some unfinished pastry or other, because they'll probably find it on their bedside table when they get home, along with a note, in colourful crayon, saying *You forgot this bit (smiley face)*.

Meanwhile, every second Wednesday, we find ourselves tapping our fingers and checking the clock to see if it's time to collect our budding chef from class. We've been conditioned, see, like Pavlov's famous dogs, to anticipate the rattle of a certain tin.

—Keen, isn't she? is what her cookery teacher might say as our daughter skips along beside her out of the classroom, obliviously mid-prattle, when I go to pick her up.

—Yes. Yes she is, is what I might reply through what I hope looks more like a grin than a grimace.

—I hope you're hungry, our little baker will warn, cheerfully buckling herself into the back seat of the car, the battered box on her lap emitting some tantalising after-oven odour.

—I could be, I'll joke. —Why?

Time was, my wife or I would take great pains to enlist the girl to help bake cookies or a cake, as an activity, to coax her away from the telly. Now it is we who are tugged to the kitchen where we're instructed that today we will 'mostly' be making banana bread, or cupcakes, or chocolate mousse.

—That's not folding, that's beating, she'll scold as one of us toils under her watchful furrowed brow, arms crossed over a pristine apron, —The recipe says *fold*.

—Yes, chef, I'll mutter.

Amazingly, she's never been put off by the occasional cooking calamity, not even the time we had to pry the whisks of a small handheld electric mixer off of her head after she leaned in too close and became entangled.

—Why do you think you're the one who does all the *folding* now? notes my wife when I remember this.

—Clever girl, I whisper, nodding slowly, eyes wide with mock awe.

—When I was little, I suddenly recall, —if I was in trouble, my parents would sometimes threaten to fetch the wooden spoon. The girl would probably just grab it, run off to the kitchen, and use it to whip up cupcakes.

—And guess who'd be the one in trouble then, if you didn't sample some of it, chuckles my wife.

—You know, I tell her, checking my watch nervously one last time before collection, then fetching plates, forks and notepaper, —because it is entirely true.

Are You It? *Really?*

—What would you like for your birthday? I ask the middle boy at the dinner table, to which he just squirms a little and shoves more bread in his mouth. —There must be something. It's a big birthday, seventeen.

—Sixteen, corrects my wife, shooting me a dark look.

—Of course, I say. —Sixteen. The age of consent! I have absolutely no idea why I said this, but now it's out there and I can feel my wife glaring at me, cutlery suspended.

—I think, corrects the eldest, —the age of consent is actually seventeen. He fiddles with his smartphone for the answer. It looks like he's throttling some small, black, shiny animal with his thumbs.

—Right, I say, clearing my throat. —Anyway…

—It's twelve in Vatican City, he chortles.

—It is never, I tell him.

—That would explain a lot, mutters my wife.

—Thirteen in Spain, he says, squinting and scrolling.

—Well, we're never going to Spain then, says my wife.

—What does 'age of consent' mean? asks the girl.

—Can you just put that down at the dinner table, I hiss at the eldest, trying to regain control of things.

—It doesn't matter, says my wife. —We are never, ever going to Spain or Vatican City.

—But I might quite like to go to Spain.

—This is all your fault, you know, I tell the eldest.

—What is? That we're not going to Spain?

I place my knife and fork on the table as if surrendering weapons. —I only wanted to know if there is any kind of present I should... That's when I notice over the din of world facts from my left, and debate over Spain from my right, that the boy whose birthday is looming has already quietly cleared his place and left.

—We should count ourselves lucky, really, says my wife later from behind a book. —He's so easy going.

He is, actually. Always has been, in fact, from the moment I first saw him lying under the hospital heat lamp. He didn't seem to cry or gawk sightlessly around like ordinary babies. He just looked directly at me, a little icily as it happens, as if to say, *Are you it? Really?*

It was, dare I say it, mildly disconcerting. I even recall joking at the time that I fully expected we'd be followed home from hospital by ravens—or, at the least, find a big black Rottweiler sitting outside our front door, growling ominously when we arrived.

—I know, I tell my wife, shaking off the image, but making a mental note to check out *The Omen* movie quadrilogy on Amazon as a possible birthday gift, —where *did* we get him?

—Well, she says quite seriously, letting her book collapse

for a moment, —*you're* the one who was supposed to be in charge of making sure he wasn't taken away, that we got the right one....

—It was a difficult birth, I mutter defensively. —I may have blacked out after, just for a minute.

I jest, of course. Our second-eldest is not the Antichrist. he's not even a very naughty boy. In fact, he has always been well-behaved: soldiering on, tolerating his family with a sort of quiet resignation. No slaughtering of babysitters or downing airplanes using only the power of his dark will, though I still might occasionally look up to catch him regarding me with a kind of cold, calm curiosity.

—Most children do that, don't they?

—Of course they do, says my wife from back behind her book again, but I'm not convinced she's listening.

—He does like horror, I fret.   I could get him some films online.

—Just do what you always do, says my wife, —and get him something that *you* would like.

Is that what I do? is what I wonder as I trundle off to search Amazon for horrors. Is that why we have all those box-set *Twilight Zone* collections and the like, stacked all the way to the ceiling? I didn't buy them *all* for myself. Did I? Is that why I get so excited about the children's birthdays? Surely not. So unfair.

I look up the original *Omen* movie only to find, though it was made in 1976, and starred Gregory Peck, and by now probably considered vintage by our lot, it's rated R 'for strong graphic violence' and 'disturbing images'.

—Hmm, I hear myself say as I fish out my credit card.

As I go around turning out lights before bed, I find the middle boy still ensconced in front of a screen clutching a PlayStation controller. I look just in time to see what appears to be a human head exploding.

— What is THAT? I say.

— It's called Fallout, he tells me.

— Can I have a go? I ask.

— I was going to bed anyway, he sighs, handing me the controls.

— Goodnight, I say after him — Damien.

Staring Straight Ahead

It's the first sunny Saturday in about nine and a half years, so we've talked the three of our sullen, six-foot, longhaired, baritone offspring and their homicidally-irritable preteen sister into a family outing.

—We're driving to the allotments, my wife instructs cheerily at a decibel level that would probably measure just below siren pitch but for the fact that she's muffled by several tons of abandoned sports gear crammed dangerously under the stairs, from where rubber boots are now being fired into the hall.

—We're ALL going, she orders amid stifled thumps and something crashing. —It'll be fun.

—I must be missing something, intones the middle boy acerbically from behind the PlayStation, —like the part that's supposed to be 'fun'.

He has a point. I'm rather dreading it myself as it happens. We haven't been to our allotment since late last

August, which was around the time we finally choked down the last courgette we could stomach, since these appeared to be the only vegetables we seemed unable to inadvertently kill.

Truth be told, it's probably taken this long to come around to the idea of returning because the last time we went up, for a mid-winter inspection, we found rat holes in the parsnip patch.

—Hedgehogs, I fibbed at the time, trying to coax my wife down from on top of the fence, —I'm sure of it.

I stuck a five-foot bamboo pole into one of the passages and promptly lost it. —Eh, perhaps we'll just come back another time, I relented, backing away slowly up the path with her on my shoulders.

—Come on, I tell everyone now, trying to sound encouraging. —I'm sure it won't kill you, I lie.

We're terrible gardeners mostly, our family, which may be why our house is entirely surrounded by cobbles and rockeries. Because otherwise we'd look like we were being overrun by a sort of starved and motley army of man-eating plants in a painfully slow-motion attack scene from *Day of the Triffids*.

One thing, however, that we *are* quite good at is dressing up in boots, flannel shirts and work gloves, like Richard Briers and Felicity Kendal in that TV series from way back in the seventies, *The Good Life*, then going up to our allotment and sitting there with a bottle of wine amid the devastation that we've wrought on the plant kingdom.

—Paradise, I'll tell my wife.

—Bounteous, she'll agree before we scoop up our basket of a few gnarled peapods, a half-hearted parsnip or two and a mean potato, then sneak off to get chips for everyone.

Refusing to be beaten, even by an army of several

hundred thousand ravenous slugs, we've coughed up the money for another year's lease, determined on our third attempt to make a proper go of it and to get the whole family involved this time as the groaning, that is, the 'growing' season, kicks off.

—Are we nearly there yet? says the eldest helpfully behind us in the car from somewhere inside all the headphones and hair. In fact, we're still waiting in the driveway with the engine running, for the eleven-year-old, who finally skips out to the car last, dressed as though she's off to a disco.

—Um, I start to say, then think better of it and we just take off.

We haven't gone far when I am forced to pull over and deliver a warning, as it is evident that the girl is ready to fling herself from her seat and claw the face off her fourteen-year-old brother, who has been methodically antagonising her from behind her headrest since we left, while the sixteen-year-old provides a rather unhelpful running commentary from the seat beside him.

The dog is barking hysterically and our eldest is just staring straight ahead, saying the word 'stop' over and over again. My wife tries to drown it all out by turning up the radio until it's deafening.

We've travelled all of about 40 meters around the green from our house at this point. —Hello, I mouth through the windscreen to a neighbour over the shrieks, howls and flailing fists behind me.

When we finally get to the allotments—really only a short drive away for normal people—each of the family immediately focuses on their separate tasks. The eldest finds a handy pile of wood on which to perch himself and begin texting with his iPhone; his two brothers stand as far away from each other as possible and start stabbing listlessly at the ground with rusted implements; the girl just wanders off singing to herself—and the dog sets about disemboweling a glove.

Living the dream, I tell my wife.

—Paradise, she deadpans.

—Can we just go back to the house without you? says the youngest teen finally. —It'll be exercise for us and a nice walk for the dog, he says, having clearly been formulating this argument for some time.

—Alright, sighs my wife, —if you all promise to...

But they're already filing out the rickety gate and disappearing up the path.

—At least they're doing something together, she says, staring after them ruefully as they go, three beanpoles of boys and their sister bouncing along behind them, crazy dog in tow.

—I suppose it's too early to go for wine, I suggest.

—I think we've probably earned it, she says and we lean on our spades for a minute, looking suitably rustic, enjoying the sudden delicious silence.

—Yes, I tell her. —I'd say we have.

One Leg Dangling By A Nerve

—I've had a slow-motion accident, reveals my wife, coming in from putting the rubbish out and looking a tad dishevelled.

—You've had a what?

—I was between the bins, she pants, clutching her arm, —and I put my foot on the wheel to give it a budge.

—A budge.

—A budge, she says, clearly becoming irritated. —Then the whole thing started tipping me up, so my other leg went in the air and I slipped between the bins...

—So you were tipped, I say, just to clarify, —and fell in the bin... but in slow motion.

—Yes, she says, rolling up a trouser leg and examining her knee for marks. —It was awful.

—Well, I tell her, turning to take in two of the boys, currently suspended in the act of spooning cereal through their fringes. —I'd like to say we shouldn't laugh, but...

One of the boys chokes on his spoon, then recovers. My wife shoots us a warning glare. I try to stifle a grin.

—What I mean is, it sounds like you've had a lucky escape. Shall I fetch the frozen peas?

I can't help but picture her helpless expression in what was surely the perfect Wile E. Coyote moment, with all the timing to hold up a sign with the word 'HELP' on it as she vanished ever so slowly from view by one drowning leg.

Lest I seem insensitive, let me just point out that no one is very charitable in our house when it comes to dishing out sympathy for another's mishaps. And there are only ever two remedies on offer in what constitutes our family first aid chest, a half empty bag of frozen peas and the offer of a liedown.

—Or would you like a lie-down?

—No, I would not, she says, straining to see her elbow.

I'd like to be able to say that our family is not really so accident prone, but the sad fact is, we are, most of us. The girl can't so much as pick up a pot while drying the dishes without inadvertently bashing herself in the face. And the youngest boy was so prone to flinging himself into walls, tables or any stationary object, that not only did we get to know every short cut to the hospital, we should have had reserved parking with our names painted on.

That said, I can't recall the middle boy ever having so much as bitten his own lip, though you wouldn't know by the painful sighs, particularly as we mime our blow-by-blow accounts of our latest painful calamities. And the eldest seems to not only have escaped childhood mercifully free of the usual collisions and cuts, he is somehow capable of shooting off to the train every morning, down the middle of an often icy road, balanced on nothing more than a wooden board with a few tiny wheels on it.

I, meanwhile, need only stroll in to the kitchen in socks, like any normal, half-dressed human, to end up hopping around, having cracked a toe on the doorframe. Naturally, I shriek as though I've caught it in a mincing machine.

—What happened? my wife will say.

—I've smashed my toe, I'll lament, rocking and cradling it. —Completely shattered it this time. No, no, no! Don't touch it.

—I'll fetch the frozen peas, she'll mutter.

—I'll be lying down, I'll sniff, hobbling away.

Of course, being a man, I am capable of withstanding extraordinary levels of pain, which my wife can attest to, since I typically give her running updates.

—Oh man, now it's really hurting. Like a bee sting, only red hot, like a knife, no wait, more like a branding iron. I think I may have chipped off a shard of bone. I only hope it doesn't enter my bloodstream. Oh sweet Jesus...

Grimly, I'll soldier on, sometimes for days, often fancying that I'm the bloke in that movie Touching the Void, who drags himself off a mountain with one leg dangling by a nerve. And this is generally my frame of mind as I eventually haul myself to the doctor, by which time I'm sure I need a specialist of some kind, if only to vindicate me with something like, 'my God man, how have you been able to withstand such pain? I prescribe the strongest pharmaceuticals available'.

What's far more likely is I'll fork out a fifty for the privilege of being told it's 'a bad bruise', 'a little swollen' or 'slightly sprained', all of little comfort to the dying.

—Perhaps you might try lying down, the doctor will say, —and putting some frozen peas on it.

—You're not writing about this in your diary, says my wife now, still rubbing her elbow and glaring.

I sense that this isn't a question.

—Of course not, I tell her defensively. —I'm writing about something else entirely. I'm writing about Wile E. Coyote… and why we hate frozen peas so much.

OCTOBER
NOVEMBER
DECEMBER
JANUARY
FEBRUARY
MARCH
APRIL
MAY
JUNE
JULY
AUGUST
SEPTEMBER
OCTOBER

Rustling Like A Giant Shopping Bag

—Nice, says my wife, —that you get to have a little time away from the family, a bit of 'man time'.

—It's not 'nice', I grumble, wrestling with a sock, —and it's not 'man time'. It's training. On a mountain. For a very difficult challenge.

—Ohhh, she says, and I watch her carefully for a moment, one foot poised awkwardly as the sock is made ready, just to see if she rolls her eyes to heaven, but she continues to gather up clothes.

—Still, she says from the bathroom now, —you'll be able to have a good natter.

I stop struggling again and heave an irritated sigh.

—We will not be 'having a good natter', we will be… clambering.

But I can hear how unconvincing I sound.

If only, I think to myself, I could call it 'mountain climbing' without having to have a helmet and a coil of rope. It's most unfair. But then I make a mental note to check with the lads to see if there's any way we might need an ice pick, as I'd quite like one, as they look really good.

—It's not 'time away from the family' either, I yell down the hall after her, pausing mid sock once more. —It doesn't count on a weekday. They're all in school.

—I'm 'family', she says, suddenly poking her head back in the door and scaring me badly: —Do I not count? Or can I come as well?

—Well, of course, you could... I suppose...

But she's already turned away again, chuckling to herself, then begins calling for the children to get up.

I'm fiddling with a flask when the little girl skips into the kitchen. —What are you doing?

—I'm getting ready for a big hike. *Hike*, I decide, sounds better, more adventurous. To hell with it. —A climb. It's a mountain climb. I may even need an ice pick. Probably.

—Cool, she chirrups and skips off again.

At last, I think as I test some of the straps on my back pack on the table in what I think is a manly way: someone who's actually talking a little sense. After all, I've made a considerable investment in sufficient gear to look suitably Ernest Shackleton for this series of weekly forays into the hills, mountains, rather, to get into shape for a six-peak hike, 'climb' that is, later in the year.

—I'm participating in a serious outdoor challenge, is what I told the bewildered assistant in the sports shop, before demanding: —Do you stock survival rations?

—We have woolly hats.

I ended up buying waterproof trousers and a monstrous pair of padded gloves almost as big as my backpack.

As I finish making my sandwiches, inspired by the single encouraging word from the girl, I go to examine the heroic figure I cut in the mirror. But with my trousers tucked into socks; waterproof gear and little rucksack; mitts resembling something my mum might have sewn into the sleeves of my anorak with elastic; sandwiches and flask, I look more Adrian Mole than Scott of Antarctica.

—Don't suppose you want to take the dog? says my wife.

Normally, the merest rustle of a jacket would be enough to induce a fit of froth-festooned barking and a hysterical, four-pawed Wall of Death circuit of the house, but today, despite all her master's noisy preparations, the dog is nowhere to be seen.

—Molly? I call, clomping across the kitchen floor in my huge boots and rustling like a giant shopping bag. It's then I notice the dog blinking balefully at me from behind the glass doors of the sitting room, where she promptly turns away in what looks like embarrassed disgust.

—Eh, best not bring her actually, I stammer. —Deer. Mountain goats. You know how it is…

—In Carlingford? she says, shaking her head.

There's a single short beep from outside.

—That's me.

I grab my gear and waddle to the front door.

—Try not to get too muddy, she says, sticking out her cheek for my kiss.

—Honestly. Getting muddy will be the least of our concerns out there.

I squint off into the horizon for emphasis as I say this.

Trudging to the car, I throw my backpack into the boot then slip into the back seat and nod to my four friends as we pootle off, waving awkwardly to my wife from behind steamed windows.

—Did you bring sandwiches? asks someone, as we turn onto the main road.

—Cheese and pickle, dash of mustard. You?

—Sausage, black pudding and relish.

—Sounds like we've just about everything we need, says someone else, plugging in a phone to the car stereo and turning up the volume as The Stones blare.

I frown over at one of the lads, remembering something and yell over the music.

—Hey, reckon we might need an ice pick at any point?

—I don't know, he yells back, —but I'd love one.

Mrs Doubtfire Was Not Pakistani

—Right, you lot, announces my wife from the bottom of the stairs with what sounds like one of those bullhorns used by angry socialists at protests, except that it's only her voice. —We're cleaning this house today.

Groans emanate from behind various electronic consoles and duvets in every room.

—Nooooo, says the little girl from a nest of cushions in front of the telly.

—Why? says the youngest boy from the playroom where he's folded in a bean bag annihilating something on a screen with his thumbs.

—Because I do not like living in filth, says my wife.

The dog gives a guilty look, shakes itself, then disappears into the kitchen, a contrail of floating hairs in its wake.

—Well, I don't mind it, says the boy.

—A few cobwebs, I offer from behind my guitar, —do sort of add character to the place.

—If there's one thing this house is not short on, says my wife, —it's character. I'm only amazed, she adds, —that the spiders around here aren't feeding on small birds.

I shudder. —I'll get the Hoover.

She goes upstairs to rally the other two, still in their beds, and I begin speed-drinking coffee directly from the pot in preparation.

—What's all the panic about? demands the middle teen irritably from behind his hair when he eventually shuffles into the kitchen. —Who's coming?

—The window washer, I tease, untangling flex and dropping bits of vacuum cleaner around the place. —You know how it is. If someone's going to be looking in the windows, your mum wants the place tidy.

—Watch yourself, she tells me as she reappears and begins doling out jobs. —Right, she tells the girl. —You're emptying the compost.

—Not the compost, she wails. —I *hate* the compost.

—Careful of the maggots, the youngest teen tells her.

—Right, you are now hoovering the stairs.

—Not the stairs, he says in pain. —Why do I always get the stairs?

—Don't forget the cobwebs. I pass him a bit of Hoover.

—Sinks, my wife instructs the middle teen's fringe.

—Ugh, it replies.

The eldest appears, looking like hair on a stick.

—You can do the windows, my wife tells him.

—Yeah, he mutters, —because that's going to happen.

—It is going to happen, says my wife, —because you're going to do it.

He heaves a sigh. —Can I just have some breakfast first?

—Sorry, she says, snatching away the cornflakes. —The kitchen closed for breakfast just before 3pm.

Eventually, they each fall to their various tasks—none of the tasks they were assigned, as it happens—and with whatever the opposite of vigour is. Rigour.

My wife ends up having to do the kitchen compost, then marches off on an errand, exasperated. The two youngest fall at each other's throats over a spray bottle and the two eldest half-heartedly push sweeping implements around, occasionally stopping to lift the hair off their faces to see what they're bumping into. It's a bit like having a heavy metal band in to do the cleaning.

—Call that sweeping? I hoot, suddenly high on coffee, in what I think is my best Mrs Doubtfire voice.

The two heaps of hair stop and blink at me.

—Mrs Doubtfire, I tell them. —Robin Williams plays a sort of cross-dressing Nanny McPhee?

—And she's Pakistani? offers the eldest.

I'm hurt. —Scottish.

—Are all your impressions from films made before we were born? says the middle teen's fringe.

—And Pakistani? says the eldest.

—You missed a bit, I say, making a wide circular motion with my finger that encompasses the entire room.

With everyone occupied, well, after a fashion, I consign myself to cobweb duty, using the longest conceivable combination of attachments to maintain as safe a distance as possible, and recoiling in disgust whenever I hear something plump being sucked up the tube.

By the time my wife gets back, which isn't long, I've suffered a caffeine crash and abandoned the vacuum cleaner on its side halfway along the hall. Wires are draped over the sideboard. There are attachments halfway up the stairs. I'm flat on my back on the floor in the sitting room.

—I'm having a moment, I explain.

—Wonderful. And the kids? Are they having a moment as well?

—If by 'kids' you mean Wednesday and Pugsley Addams, and the pair from Metallica? Probably.

—I don't ask for much, she sighs, suddenly sitting on my stomach and making me utter an involuntary 'woof'.

—You really don't, I groan.

—Just a little family effort. A clean sink or two, a small path through the debris…

—It's not a lot, I wheeze with my remaining breath.

—But you're probably right… She looks around then gets up with a last gratuitous bounce. —A few cobwebs never harmed anyone.

—Honestly? I whisper hoarsely, massaging my ribcage and struggling to my feet. —I don't think the spiders could survive long around here with all this dog hair anyhow.

She grins. —Everything's just crap, isn't it?

I grin back. —Shedloads of character though.

She kicks the door closed and I reach for the remote.

One Catastrophe At A Time

Bloody hell, is all I can think, opening one bleary eye from a near diabetic coma after an Easter spent, as usual, rifling through the debris of decimated chocolate wrappers. —Ack! is what I actually croak, or something like it, as the full horror of how I'm to spend my holiday Monday materialises beneath the pillow I now clutch to my face.

—There's sewage all over the garden, continues my wife in full throttle from somewhere in the hall, like a radio correspondent witnessing the Hindenburg disaster. —Nobody flush anything! she orders.

She pokes her head in. —We still have those rods, don't we? Then she continues as if from a bullhorn from the landing: —It's bubbling up EVERYWHERE.

—Nnnrrrgh, I wince, recalling hours spent plunging a filthy manhole just months ago, sweating and gagging as I forced twenty yards of poles into the obscene burbling foam, as though giving the entire housing estate some sort of giant, hideous enema.

—*And we're out of milk as well,* yells my wife from downstairs now.

—One catastrophe at a time, for the love of God, I mutter, shuffling down to the kitchen.

—April fool! she announces brightly.

I lurch over to the back door to see for myself and am almost delirious with relief.

—You mean, I say, clutching my head and trying to fathom, —we're not even out of milk?

—Mm-hmm, she grins, producing two full bottles and adding: —Best of all? They're not dyed purple.

Before our children became irritable mutes requiring an impending nuclear attack just to consider getting out of bed before lunchtime, we'd come down on April Fools' Day to find not just milk, but every fluid in the fridge, dyed with food colouring, then spend days trying to go about our business with freakish neon lips.

—I was going to tell the boys, confesses my wife, —we'd had that banjaxed PlayStation fixed and it was back early from the repair shop. That would get them up soon enough.

—Hmm, I tell her. —Playing with fire with that one.

—I know. They mightn't talk to us for days.

—As opposed…

She chuckles, puts down her coffee, tip-toes to the stairs and shouts: —BOYS!

Later, showered and dressed, I wonder how best to spend a little of the day that, for a while at least, I'd been sure was doomed to be a reeking, retching hell.

—I think I'll clean the fish tank, I announce, looking over at the glutinous green tank of gurgling algae in the corner. My way of giving something back, I decide.

—Really? says my wife, like this might be another April Fools' Day hoax.

—Really, I tell her.

—You'll need to put down newspapers… she says doubtfully.

—I know about the newspapers, I say.

She escapes on some errands and by the time I've kitted myself out and am cautiously approaching the aquarium with jugs and hose, I feel like Dan Aykroyd in *Ghostbusters*, then I plunge a hand into the gelatinous gloop and feel around for 'Moustachio', the bottom-feeder we've had for years, he who has withstood many a long vacation by seeming to feast on the remains of his less hardy cousins.

—What we have here, I seethe, trying to coax the thing into a receptacle, —is what we refer to as a focused, non-terminal repeating phantasm, or a Class Five full roaming vapor. Real nasty one, too.

I run out of *Ghostbusters* quotes by the time I actually manage to empty everything, clean it all and begin replacing all the water, all mercifully without incident. It's only as I go to put Moustachio back, that to my horror, he makes a leap for it, thrashing down behind the tank amongst the power cables.

—GOD, I shriek a little too high, then fumble around for his slippery, flopping body, eventually getting hold, and plopping him in where he sinks like a stone, then after that, just sort of drifts along the bottom on the current like a corpse before wedging conspicuously under a bit of a rock.

—JESUS, I wheeze, clutching the sides of the tank just as the front door open and my wife arrives in.

I jam the lid on and ball up the newspapers off the floor.

—Done, I chirrup, grimacing.

—Great, says my wife, coming over and leaning on her knees to look. —How's Moustachio?

—Healthy as a whistle, I stammer. —Clean as an ox. But when the coast is clear, I reach in with a pencil and give him a prod.

He just sort of bobs sideways a bit on one rigid fin.

I spend hours agonizing. The one bloody time I bother to clean that cursed tank and I manage to kill a family pet that's at least half the age of our youngest child.

I wait all evening for someone to notice, rehearsing things like 'well, he was fine earlier'. I'm wracked with guilt. It's my wife who finally looks.

—Nice to actually be able to see Moustachio again.

—He's just sleeping, I blurt.

—Well, he's having a nice dream, she says, —because he's bombing around the place.

—Bastard! I say before I can help myself, then promptly confess the whole thing

—Looks like you've been had twice today, chortles my wife. —Fool.

—Just wait, I tell her. —Next year. You and that conniving little fish.

Stupid Tears

—Doesn't anyone answer the phone around here? is what I grumble as the handset near me in the office upstairs where I'm working chirrups on its cradle for the umpteenth time today. It's a freezing, blustery midweek April afternoon and I'm already irritated with myself for letting a myriad of minor deadlines mount up. My wife is talking to someone at the front door, the children are home from school and, wherever they are in the house, I figure someone must be close enough to a phone.

But it's my wife who picks up. —Sure. I'll just get him, I hear her say and I wince, exasperated, at the footsteps on the stairs. —It's your sister, she says.

—Mom's in hospital, says the voice in the receiver before I can say anything. —It's serious.

My throat clicks. Our mother is in America where she has lived for more than twenty years, eight of them in the shadow of an inoperable aneurysm.

—Look, we knew this day would come, says my sister, or something like it. —But she can talk. They're making her as comfortable as they can. You should call. Here's the number of the hospital.

The prefix is familiar and dialling on autopilot I reach her house by mistake where the phone rings off and my heart plummets as I think of how it's been weeks since I last bothered to call.

Dialling again, I reach the hospital and a Midwestern drawl: —Are you family? to which I hear myself stammer: —It's her son, in Ireland.

—Hello? says mom a moment later. She seems impossibly calm, anything but elderly, the same voice I've known since I first learned to speak.

—How… are you? I try.

—Oh, she says, and I want to think it's a small, weak laugh she's fighting. —Not so good, I guess.

—So how serious is this? I say, like it's something I can fix from almost four thousand miles away. —Is there anything they can do?

—I s'pose we'll see what happens, is what she says. —How's things over there?

—Busy, I say, flailing around the cluttered office and shuffling papers. —I've been sending my columns, I suddenly blurt, meaning *I'm sorry it's been so long since we've talked.* —Did you get them?

—I got two on Saturday, she says with heartbreaking warmth. —I read every word. How's everything else?

—It's cold here, but I think the sun's coming out, I say, because I can't think of anything else and this can't possibly be one of the last times I'll talk to her.

I realise I've forgotten to breathe. —So, I manage, —What's next?

—Well, we just do the best we can, she says. —Just know that I love you.

—Um, same, I gulp, then: —Talk soon. And I put the phone down.

Downstairs the dog barks, our youngest is teasing her with a treat. I call my sister back.

—She sounded fine, I tell her. —Do you think she'll be okay?

—I'm sorry, says my sister gently. —I thought you understood.

It hits me. The time bomb in her chest has gone off and, there's really no other way of putting it, mom's life is trickling away.

When we're done talking, I tell my wife.

—You should call the hospital again, she says, which I do, because I really don't want our last conversation to be about the weather.

This time, I hiss in my head, say something important.

—Hi again, is what I end up warbling like an idiot.

—Hello love, she says.

—So, uh, will you be going home?

—Well, I'll be going somewhere, she says.

Silence.

—Hey, I say, half aware that I've been punching my leg. —Remember when I was small? One time… I woke up in the middle of the night, afraid… and we went downstairs and had cookies and milk in the dark by the stove, one ring lit to keep us warm…

—Oh, she says, confused momentarily, then: —That *was* a long time ago.

—Well, I still remember that sometimes, I tell her, hating the stupid tears that shoot out so hard they miss my face.

—Well, she says. —You take care.

—Should I come? I offer, knowing there's probably not enough time and I'd just be another worry.

—Oh, no, don't do that, she says, meaning it. —I love you, she says. —I'll see you soon.

My wife tells the boys what's been going on. Our little girl is still oblivious, which is both heart-rending and wonderful. The mood in the house is otherwise quiet and watchful. We wait.

I fish out ingredients from the cupboard and make cookies, filling the night air with the comforting smells of baking, then I bring some in to everyone before they've cooled, which seems to cheer everyone. up just a little.

Returning to the kitchen for mine, I light one ring on the cooker and turn the lights out, standing with a glass of milk, munching alone in the gloom.

~~OCTOBER~~
~~NOVEMBER~~
~~DECEMBER~~
~~JANUARY~~
~~FEBRUARY~~
~~MARCH~~
~~APRIL~~
(MAY)
JUNE
JULY
AUGUST
SEPTEMBER
OCTOBER

Forgetting To Suck It In

We're hovering between family crises when an old friend who's from Russia looks us up and comes to stay.

For my wife and me, it's a welcome excuse to put our worries on hold for a day or two, to relive some old times, to recall the people we once were. But the teenagers don't seem quite convinced.

—Who? says the eldest suspiciously, like he must have misheard us the first time.

—Why? mutters another glumly as he helps his brother drag a mattress from the loft. The boys will all have to bunk in together for a few days, an idea which they seem to be having a little trouble becoming accustomed to.

But my wife and I are already obliviously digging out dusty albums of old photos of our former selves, from an age ago—that age being BC, or Before Children.

—Look, I say to them, pointing excitedly to a page of blurry prints, —that's the house your mother and I lived in before you were born.

—Your hair looks weird, the little girl tells me.

—It was the eighties, I pout defensively, but squinting to see.

—Actually, it was the nineties, says my wife from behind a heap of freshly laundered guest towels now.

—Your shirt has flowers on it, observes one of the boys as he's passing, like he's telling me the zipper on my trousers is down.

—I'm pretty sure that's paisley, I say, squinting harder at the page.

—It's definitely flowers, says the girl solemnly from underneath her eyebrows, like she's breaking the news of some sort of embarrassing illness.

—I loved that shirt, I mutter to no-one in particular, adding, —I look like Tom Cruise, and ignoring it when everyone pauses in their tracks for a second to roll their eyes patronisingly.

—*Cocktail* was a very popular movie, I'll have you know, I announce, snapping the album closed.

—*Cocktail* was the eighties, says my wife from the hall. —That photo is from the nineties.

—So it was a few years before I got around to watching it on video, I say.

—What's video? says the girl.

I go to the airport alone to meet our friend, sucking my stomach in every time someone comes through the door marked 'Arrivals' and letting it flop over my belt again every time it's not him.

I've forgotten to suck it in again when he finally appears. We slap each other on the back and look each other up and down.

—You look the same, he lies, beaming.

—So do you, I lie back.

There's a tiny child perched on his luggage cart.

—Michelle, says my friend, —say hello.

It's difficult at first to get my head around the idea of our one-time bachelor friend being a father, a single father as it turns out. But I can only imagine what it's like for him to see us being towered over by three tall teens.

—Unbelievable, is what he says when we finally sit down together in the kitchen.

His little girl takes ours away but the boys hang around on the outskirts of the room as we open wine.

—I remember, he says, —when you both lived in that house on the lake, with the boat.

—You had a house, says the youngest teen disbelievingly from the doorframe, —on a lake, with a boat?

—In America, I manage, reeling pleasantly with the nostalgia for a moment.

—And we all went on jet skis when I visited, continues our friend.

—You went on jet skis? says the middle boy, emphasising the words 'you' and 'jet skis' dubiously.

—We did, says my wife, looking at me, smiling and adding: —It was fun, too.

—Your father, confides our friend mischievously, —once sang *Twist And Shout,* on top of a bar, in a casino.

The boys bury their faces in their hands.

That night, I dig out a flowery shirt before dinner. It's not quite the one from the photo album, or the movie, but when we invite more friends around to join us, one of them knows Tom Cruise's speech from *Cocktail* all the way through, and we make Cosmopolitans with ice and a shaker and howl with laughter.

The kids listen on the fringes with what seems like a mixture of horror and fascination at the bizarre idea that their parents once had a life without children or responsibilities, a life in which people dressed in outlandish clothes and did silly things.

And it's a blissful few hours, in which we all forget about things like notes for school, study regimes, taxes, mortgages and household bills, as wine bottles empty and candles burn out around us, and the table becomes littered with old photos of skinny young people bearing our faces.

The next day it's all still waiting for us, however, and it almost seems odd to be back being parents again after having been off travelling with our friend in a time machine.

—It's good, I think, says our friend, tying the laces on his little girl's shoes over breakfast, —this, he says, motioning around us with his eyes before adding: —being parents.

—Yeah, I smile over the clatter of cereal bowls and last-minute searches for schoolbooks and locker keys, the familiar morning cacophony around us. —And it's kind of good to remember when we were 'real people', too.

Officially A Jerk

—Haven't you got some homework to do? I ask irritably without looking up as the girl loiters lankily around the kitchen island while I'm trying to chop vegetables and listen to music. —You're in the way of my multitasking.

—I've done my homework, but I have extra.

—Oh? I say, meaning *shouldn't you be getting on with it?*

—Yeah, she says, drawing an invisible line along the countertop in a way that signals an imminent and lengthy explanation.

—Alright, I say, putting down a carrot and wiping my hands on a cloth, —I give up. Why do you have 'extra'?

—Well, I was supposed to do some research on the internet, which I did, but my teacher said I didn't do it properly, so she gave me extra work.

—And what were you supposed to research?

—It was about how the indigenous people of the rain forest dress, the sorts of things they wear. I looked it up and Yahoo Answers said that the people of the rainforest wear hats and coats and gloves.

—Oh, come on. That's just someone messing. Your teacher is right. You obviously didn't research it right. Why would someone in the rainforest need a coat and gloves?

—For when it snows. That's what it said and the person who answered the question said the reason they know is because they actually live in a rainforest… in Canada.

—What's up? says my wife, coming in to see my jaw suspended in mid air.

—Our brilliant daughter has extra homework because her extensive research into the clothing customs of indigenous rainforest dwellers has revealed that they dress… like Canadians.

I give my wife what I think is a suitably comic look of utter incredulity. —There's still a place on my pub quiz team for another member, you know, I add.

—She did her best, says my wife sympathetically, which is when I notice for the first time that the lanky girl, who suddenly seems smaller again, is leaning on her elbows, forehead creased, hand hiding a rapidly crumpling lip.

—Oh, come on, I say. —Really?

—She has a lot of work to do and she's tired. Come on, I'll help you. My wife takes her to the other side of the kitchen where they begin tugging huge books out of a schoolbag, and I'm left gawping down at my stupid pile of vegetables and hating myself for being such a jerk.

Hours later, we sit down to tacos. It's my attempt at cheering things up, having ditched the half-chopped carrots.

—Bo Diddley, I announce, between mouthfuls.

—Sorry? sighs the eldest, looking at me wearily, like I'm some sort of harmless lunatic at a bus stop.

I'm doing what I think is my impressive trick of being able to name the artist just as the next song begins. The youngest teen gets up, on cue, and goes over to check the iPod.

—Yup, he says, sitting down again.

—Yesss, I say, punching the air. —Mastermind eat your heart out. I'm telling you. I am that good.

—Uh, says the middle teen from behind his hair, —isn't this your music list we're listening to?

The little girl snorts involuntarily from behind a napkin, the first sound she's made in an hour.

—Yeah, I say defensively, —but it's on shuffle, so...

—So, just to be clear, says the eldest, —your chosen specialist subject is guessing your own music collection.

—Extremely specialist actually, I tell him.

—Wow. Impressive. Good luck with the pub quiz.

—I'll have you know, I start to explain, —that my team came in second place on the very first night I joined.

—Before that, they'd always won, my wife butts in helpfully. —Your dad helped break a record.

—Just because you're right, I mutter, only half jokingly, —doesn't make you clever.

—Words of wisdom at last, she lobs back.

—I hate my whole family, I tell this to my taco.

After we clear up, the girl begins hoisting books back onto the table again rather dejectedly.

—So, all this extra work you have, what's it on? I ask.

—The brain, she pouts.

—How apt, I tell her.

—What do you mean? she says.

—Might I suggest a little research? I take a book from her hand, sliding it back into her bag and winking at her mother. —Such as, the effects of ice cream and *The Simpsons* on a little girl's brain?

—Okayyyy? She giggles suspiciously.

—And when you hand in your work to the teacher tomorrow morning, I tell her, as we make a balancing act of our bowls and spoons and take them into the TV room, —don't forget to give her a photo of your dear old Dad.

—Why would I want to do that? she grins, her eyes glittering.

—Why, as a scientific example of course, I say, —of someone without any brains in his head whatsoever.

Don't Touch Me!

For the guts of eighteen years, my wife and I have been relentlessly dogged by one diminutive chattering parrot or another, from room to room, up and down every street, around every supermarket aisle, haunted by high-pitched anecdotes. As one grew up and into another room, another took their place. *Uh huh. Yup. You don't say,* we'd offer fruitlessly. *Don't you have something else to do? No? Really? Okay,* we'd sigh. *Mmm-hmm. Yup. Wow.* It's been an endless barrage of leapfrogging non-sequiturs, brain-numbing and exhausting; a catalogue of the startlingly obvious; a falsetto, two-foot high running commentary.

And God help us if we didn't pay attention. We'd risk being thumped or yelled at. These were monologues at gunpoint. Listen or else. We prayed for 'wine o'clock', heaving huge sighs of relief at the final gentle click of a bedroom light, leaving the bedroom door ajar as instructed, then sneaking down stairs, flinching at every creaking floorboard and finally exchanging exhausted grimaces.

We'd gone from celebrating our children's first little garbled salvos, to praying for a ceasefire.

Quite when it all flipped around, I can't say, but at some point, my wife and I became the irritant, the interruption, the presence to be wearily tolerated or escaped from.

Of course, I'm thinking none of this as the girl, the last of our four still able to communicate in anything other than a series of barely intelligible clicks and grunts, follows me around the kitchen reciting the lines from a forthcoming school play—but for the first time in I don't know how long, I actually sit down and look at her little face for a minute, revelling in the chatter.

—You're not listening. Okay, I'll start again. Ready?

I grin and off she goes again, and for the life of me, I haven't the first clue what she's on about. It doesn't really matter. I find I'm rather enjoying the chirp of her voice, her oblivious enthusiasm.

Suddenly aware she's stopped, I begin clapping.

—Awesome, I say.

—I'm not done yet. I'm just thinking of the next bit.

—Oh. I folding away my smile and hide my arms.

—Now I have to start AGAIN. She's irritated now, all but stamping one foot. She takes a deep breath and begins to rattle off her little speech again.

Halfway through this delivery, a hairy sixteen-year-old ghost glides by.

—Where are you going? I call after it.

—Out.

—Who with?

—No one.

—Wear a jack... But the door slams before I finish.

126

I look back at the kitchen counter, but it's empty.

I try to pry her away from the television where she's heaped behind a rather sour expression, but she seems to have decided to abandon any further attempts at dialogue for the time being.

—Shh. She hisses. —I'm trying to watch this.

Suddenly at a loose end, I go and bother her fourteen -year-old brother in the other room, who I find wearing a headset and busily obliterating something on a screen.

—Hey.

—What. He looks up blankly from behind his fringe and presses a button on his headset which makes a blue light on it disappear, but I can't think of anything to tell him, so I just make a face and stagger towards him with my arms out.

—Go away, he says. —I'm doing something.

—Maybe I can help. Are there zombies involved?

—Please. He says, turning away and switching the blue light on again. —Just go away.

—Come on. I put on my Dr Evil voice from Austin Powers and lurch toward him again. —Just one hug.

—Don't touch me. He ducks.

—Come on. I keep doing the voice. —Give your daddy a freakin' hug… Hug! Hug! Hug! Hug!

—Get out, he shouts. He turns away, disappears back behind his hair and into his game.

I wilt a little, watching him for a second as he rattles the controller in his hands, gasps *Aw!* into his headset as something explodes on the screen, then I turn around and shuffle off robotically, shoulders sagging a little this time.

As a last resort, I dig out my phone and text the eldest,

who's been doing college exams in the city.

How did it go today? I type, then: *Will you be home for dinner?*

Fine, comes the response, and *No.*

When my wife comes home, we pour wine and sit in the empty kitchen.

—Where is everyone? she says.

—Oh, I tell her, a little miserable, —you know. I motion around the house with my chin.

—Nice to have a bit of peace, she says, sipping.

—Yeah. I weigh up the years on invisible scales in the air with my eyes then raise my glass. —I guess.

Sex Education The South Park Way

Our eleven-year-old daughter has just completed her first sex education class, or something like it—it's difficult to know exactly, as she doesn't seem to want to talk about it.

—Go away, she says from behind her bedroom door, and —I don't want to talk about it.

We achieve inordinate amusement from her agony.

—It's about the changes that happen to your body, whispers my wife, who's with me on the landing. She silently mouths the words 'changes' and 'body'.

—Shut uuuup! moans the door.

I can't help teasing. —You mean the changes that happen to *my* body? Like how her Dad is beginning to look a little like he may be expecting twins? Why on earth would they want to teach children that? No wonder she won't come out.

A crack opens in the door. —I won't come out because you're annoying me.

She disappears.

—She had to colour in the 'changes' on a picture, continues my wife.

—A picture?

—An illustration of some kind.

—Crayon or pencil? I say. Cross-hatch or shading?

The bedroom door bursts open and the little girl growls as she pushes past and into the bathroom, where the door slams shut again. —DRAW. We had to DRAW on it.

—I did something similar at her age.

—Really? says my wife. —Do tell.

—I drew the, eh, 'changes'… all over the people in my Irish book. When my teacher found out, I was sent home with a note.

In fact, as I explain to my wife later in the kitchen where we're perched on stools on either side of the island, I was presented with a book when I was around twelve. It was called *Boys Growing Up*.

—The title of which you studiously chose to ignore.

—It was a little ironic, I say, ignoring her, —because the last thing I wanted to know about was boys growing up. I'd much rather have had a copy of *Girls Growing Up*.

—Is that so.

—But what did I get instead? A horrible book full of split anatomical drawings showing all the whatsits and doohickeys and how all the tubes were supposed to work.

—Doohickeys? Really.

—Doohickeys. With little arrows all over them. I swear, it was like a cross between a butcher's window and an Ikea flat-pack assembly pamphlet.

—That explains… so much.

—Frankly, it was terrifying.

—Well, I suspect things have moved on a tad since.

—I should hope so. I think I learned more about sex from Benny Hill.

—Like I said, *sooo* much…

—I wonder should we have some sort of extra chat, you know…

I point upstairs with a little jab of my chin.

—If by 'we' you mean 'you', then be my guest.

I think I see her stifling a smile.

—I don't recall having to have any sort of conversation with the boys about, you know, *those sorts of things*.

—Thank heavens.

—I mean, drawing a few arrows and doohickeys with a crayon on a handout with a cross-section of something like a side of beef depicted on it, is hardly going to protect the world from STDs and teenage pregnancies.

A tall mop of hair suddenly passes through the kitchen on the way to the front door with a rucksack on its back.

—I'm going out.

The voice is deeper than mine, which is discomfiting.

—Wear a condom! I yell after him.

—Jesus, he says. —I'm only going out to meet my friend… Mark.

—Better safe than sorry.

My wife glares at me. —Bring a jacket in case it rains. She shouts this just as the front door slams.

—A jacket full of condoms! I shout.

—Actually, she says as the house settles, —you did have 'that conversation' with the boys. Well, that is to say, you did what you always do.

—And what's that?

—You followed each of them through the house taunting them until they locked themselves away somewhere.

—That's not taunting. That's *South Park*… you know…

131

'When a man loves a woman, and a woman loves a man…
well, actually, sometimes the man doesn't really LOVE the
woman? But he acts like he does because he wants to get a
little action?' Chef sings it to Cartman.

—Very helpful.

—You can learn a lot from *South Park*.

—So, if any of the kids have questions or concerns about
sex, relationships or the way their bodies are suddenly
changing like a scene from *An American Werewolf in
London*, they should…

—Consult the *South Park* box set.

—I'm going to go lock myself in a room now.

—I seem to have that effect on people. Okay, so maybe
sex education is best left to the experts.

—Or anyone else but you.

I surrender. —Or that.

Secretly, I'm relieved.

She'd Run Away Screaming

We're getting a cleaner, though I don't like the word 'cleaner'. It conjures up some sort of housemaid in uniform, while we jolly well swan off in the Bentley to play golf. I hate golf. So, we're getting 'someone in to help clean house each week', much to the bewilderment of the teens.

—Why? asks the middle one. He puts a petulant upward inflection on the word which irritates me.

—Because? I enunciate in a tone that perfectly mocks his. —Our house? Is a wreck?

—I don't want a cleaner, says the youngest boy from his machine-gunner's nest in the sitting room.

—You're not getting one, my wife tells him.

—She's not a 'cleaner', anyway, I wince. —She's Aga.

—What's she going to do? he says, eyes glued to the carnage being unleashed with his thumbs.

—All the things you lot aren't, says my wife.

—Well, I don't want anyone in my room, he mutters.

—We wouldn't wish your room on anyone, I point out, swatting at him. —In fact, we've already warned her over the phone that we have a crazy person living here and not to go near their door, no matter how bad the smell.

—You can look after your own room, interjects my wife, suddenly announcing: —You can ALL look after your own rooms.

—And if you don't look after them, I add hoarsely, —we'll send in The Cleaner.

I emphasize the last two words like I'm talking about Harvey Keitel's character in Pulp Fiction, pulling one earphone out of his ear as I do this.

—Get off, he says, wriggling away.

—In the meantime, calls my wife from the hall now, —you can all help by tidying up before she comes.

—Um, why do we need to tidy up if someone is coming to clean? says the middle boy.

—Because no one, says my wife, —needs to know just how awful a pigsty we really live in.

—She'd run away screaming, I say.

—So, just to get this straight, he deadpans from the kitchen doorframe. —We now have to tidy even more than we already do, because someone is coming to clean the house each week.

—Bullseye, chimes his mother.

I applaud slowly.

—Hand that young man the giant furry giraffe.

The boy disappears, muttering.

The girl bounces in. —Can I have my hair cut? For the cleaner? She hands us a photo. —Like this.

—This is a picture of your brother, blinks my wife.

—He looks like KD Lang, I tell her.

—Who? says the youngest.

—Never mind, I tell her. —We'll still love you.

—Maybe, adds her mother. —Have a think about it.

The girl shrugs and skips off down the hall.

—She can always adopt, I say dreamily, for which I receive a jab in the ribs.

The phone rings, startling us both. It's Aga, wondering if she can come by to pick up the spare key, have a quick look around and see where the cleaning supplies are kept, the vacuum cleaner and so on.

—Cleaning supplies? says my wife when I hang up.

—Well the vacuum cleaner is easy, I say, opening the door to under the stairs and promptly triggering an avalanche of old boots, bags and several dilapidated kites inextricably intertwined with everything.

—Look, I'll deal with this, sighs my wife, wrestling a Wellington boot out of my hands.

—Right, I say. I'll go and organise my music.

—Because Aga is really going to notice that your records are alphabetical?

—Not alphabetical, I whisper as though imparting a secret, —Autobiographical.

When the bell rings, I open the door. It's Aga.

—Hello, she smiles.

—Thank heavens you're here, I say, ushering her in. —So many... change their minds at the front gate.

—Pay no attention to him, smiles my wife, shooting me a look. —Good to see you, Aga.

We show her from room to room, skirting quickly past the problem areas and arriving to the cupboard door under the stairs. My wife opens it and I flinch. The vacuum is stacked neatly in its own space. I poke my head in to the dark and blink.

—Hey, it's carpeted in here, I muffle. —Who knew?
When I extract my head again, my wife is thin-lipped.
—Uh, the vacuum, I mutter, pointing. —Is… here.
—Don't worry, my wife tells Aga. —I'll make sure he's
never here when you're around.

OCTOBER
NOVEMBER
DECEMBER
JANUARY
FEBRUARY
MARCH
APRIL
MAY
JUNE
JULY
AUGUST
SEPTEMBER
OCTOBER

You're All Walking

We're taking a family holiday soon. A proper one. Where we all go away. Together. Abroad. Me, my wife, the 'lodger', the two middle ones, all their hair, and Disco Girl.

The full potential horror of this cannot be overstated.

—We're renting a car there, announces my wife.

—Oh, I say. What I mean is 'oh dear' because we're not really our best as a family when strapped in seats, inches from each other, knees bunched, and bodies tensed into knots lest they touch even slightly, while confined to a metal box the size of a generous toilet cubicle for, well, forever. On previous trips, they'd construct peace walls out of baggage and blankets to prevent all-out war breaking out, for a while at least. But, sooner or later, someone's knee or elbow would stray into enemy territory and the whole situation would go nuclear in a matter of minutes, forcing the driver to pry their fingernails out of the steering wheel, indicate, pull over safely, and begin screaming.

137

Which is really all rather embarrassing, I'll be first to admit: a grown man losing it like that, spittle flying as the family cowers, rear left passenger door finally opening slowly and one sullen teen or other being forced to stand at the side of the road as the car takes off for another ten yards, jerks to a halt, rear left passenger door opening again and said teen allowed back in on strict probation.

And like this, slowly and painfully, we work our way around the green outside our house and, if the stars are in correct alignment, we perhaps even manage eventually to pull out onto the main road.

This is what goes through my mind as I croak through a death-mask grimace: —How *big* a car?

Like it matters how big the car is. It could be an entire tour bus travelling the length of a parking lot and our mob would still manage to devise new and ever more cruel ways to wage psychological warfare upon one another. Honestly, the CIA could take a leaf or two from behind the fogged windows of our family conveyance. If ever they wished to truly pry open the mind of the most otherwise impervious Guantanamo Bay inmate, all they'd need do is make him the driver of a twelve-year-old navy-blue five-door Alhambra carrying three hormonal and highly territorial teens and one sociopathic eleven-year-old girl. If the UN treaty on human rights even permitted it to start with, which I sincerely doubt, before they could so much as fetch a pencil the poor soul would have given up everything he knows—the illustrated version.

—Oh, I should think we should all be able to squeeze into something fairly cheap, says my wife.

Truth is, we very well could. I've seen the way our boys can fold up their nine-foot limbs like collapsible measuring sticks until they look like two sets of toes poking out of a hairstyle when they want to immerse themselves into a beanbag in front of the PlayStation for fourteen hours.

Unfortunately, leg room or lack of it is not the issue. It's how far we'll manage to get without losing all our faculties (forget about our dignity, we gave that up years ago), that's what is at stake.

—Perhaps we could all just rent bicycles instead.

My wife lobs me a sideways glance. —It's hundreds of miles from the airport to where we're going.

—Still, I say. —Think positively. If we pedal hard, they mightn't be able to catch up.

—It's nice countryside where we're going, she says, ignoring me. —I think it'll be lovely to drive around.

Yes, because the scenery matters when your offspring are clawing each other's faces off. I've only recently managed to finally begin forgetting the finer details of a driving holiday in the States almost four years ago. *'Look at the bloody scenery!'* is probably the polite version of what I shrieked in one of my less shining moments as a caring, respectable parent.

But perhaps this time *will* be different. Maybe it *will* be 'nice' and 'lovely' and other words like that, words you might associate with butterflies and smiley faces, unlike words such as 'murder' or 'maiming'.

Perhaps it will be like the movie National Lampoon's American Vacation—the rib-tickling bits, you know, before Chevy Chase loses his rag and roars at his bewildered youngsters *'We're all gonna have so much fun we'll need plastic surgery to remove our goddamn smiles!'*

Who am I kidding? It'll be a year before any of us is talking to each other again once we get back.

—I think I need wine, I manage weakly. —You?

She glares at me. —It's 8.00 in the morning.

—You're right, I tell her. —If we're dropping the kids to school, we should probably only have the one.

—Very funny, she says, but we both look the same way at the car keys sitting on the hall stand, like it's a big spider squatting there staring back at us.

—Hey kids! We both yell this at the same time, possibly because this is by no means the first time that our inner dialogue has brought us to this moment.

—You're all walking today!

Preaching To The Converted

It's the middle of Summer exams but I'm the one who feels a bit like I'm revising for a test… on a class I've been skipping all year.

—How's your French? I say to the middle teen as, in my defense, I wait for the very first cup of the coffee of the day to work its magic.

The heap of hair swivels sideways at me from across the kitchen where it's been rifling through sheaves of dog-eared notes. —I don't do French, it mutters witheringly.

—That's not the sort of attitude that will get you into college, I slurp, but I suspect this attempt at dry humour is probably a little too early for anyone.

It heaves a sort of resigned sigh, not dissimilar to one the dog emits at the front window when the postman fails to show, and I can't help but think for a second that I am a terrible disappointment.

He picks up the same books and papers over again and

throws them down in a heap when my wife steams cheerily into the kitchen.

—I need a calculator, he announces.

—I could have found you a calculator, I blurt, like it's the one question on the test I could have got right had it been on the paper at all.

My wife rolls her eyes my way, but thankfully, I can't help thinking, not because of me for once.

—You have to leave the house for your exam, she tells him, motioning to her wrist where, for the life of me, I don't think she's worn a watch in years, —in fifteen minutes, and *now* you tell me you need a calculator.

—He could have told *me*, I mumble into my coffee.

—I had one, he says accusingly. —It was right here.

We all look at the huge mess of books at one end of the room, with the piles of discarded school shoes and coats on the floor in front of it.

—Oh, well then…

The youngest teen trundles in.

—Can we go in the car?.

—You can if you ask in French, I say. He pulls his fringe aside to glare at me. —You… do French, don't you?

—You can all walk, yells my wife from halfway up the stairs now. —It'll help clear your head before your exams.

She appears moments later with a desk calculator the size of a phone directory, one of those ones with a prong sticking up where you're supposed to put a receipt roll.

—You'll have to plug it in, she says handing it to the bewildered one who's given up rummaging in the corner and is now standing with his mouth hanging open.

—Can anyone spell 'incredulous'? I pipe.

—It's this or the miniature bank calculator built in to my coin purse, says my wife. —Take it or leave it.

142

—I need a scientific calculator, he whimpers.

—Please can we just go in the car, says the hairstyle beside him. —I have an exam in, like, ten minutes.

—You've both completely failed in getting up in time and being ready, says my wife, as they both stand there looking helpless. —Come on then, she capitulates. —We'll see if the stationery shop is open.

They take off in the car and arrive back seconds later in reverse, hairstyle number one skittering in to rummage in the corner again.

—Now what have you lost?

—My jacket. It was here. On the floor. With the rest.

—Have you tried the coat rack?

This only earns me another withering look. But he looks. And it's there.

When my wife arrives back some time later, she joins me at the kitchen island from where I haven't budged through all the fuss.

—The shop was closed, she says, —so he had to make do with my coin-purse calculator.

—There's only so much one can do.

I swirl the last few coffee grounds in my mug.

—I've bought three scientific calculators in as many months, she says.

—Like I say...

—Does not really caring, make us bad parents?

—Monsters.

—It's just, she says, shaking sugar from a dispenser into a cup, —I think I used up all of my worry last year.

—You're preaching to the converted, I mutter, nodding. Last year, the eldest, who only recently finished his first year in college and so doesn't emerge from his bedroom for breakfast until after three, was immersed in the Leaving Cert. At the same time his younger brother was doing the Junior Cert.

—Just for this one year, she says, —before all the hell starts again, I feel they can bloody well organise themselves for a change. I'm on a year out.

—It's good practice for them.

—We can start worrying about the real exams again in September, she says, adding in a serious tone: —You know that means we'll have one doing the Leaving Cert and one doing the Junior Cert, at the same time, AGAIN.

—Heaven help us, I say and we both stare at the crumbs on the counter in reverential silence for a few moments.

—What I want to know is why he needs a scientific calculator for French.

—You... She pokes the air at me with a spoon: —will be out on your ear.

A Machine-Gun Loaded With Paintballs

It's easy to see how the lunatic jabbering, occasional ear-shattering shrieks and pounding of fists off a clattering table of dancing cutlery, just across the room from where we're all perched for dinner, might be considered disturbing to the average family restaurant experience. To my wife and I, however, after consecutive years of dining debacles spanning the early lives of our four, it's music to our ears, the merry refrain of which, even after all this time, as a fork now flies through the air and narrowly misses the eye of a ducking waiter, is: *Not. Our. Child.*

It's like a bizarre reenactment of the basement bunker scene in 'Downfall' where the deranged dictator lets loose a hail of psychopathic spittle over his hand-wringing generals as they try to dig a hole in the concrete with their toenails into which to disappear, only it's being played out here by a pre-schooler upon its mortified parents.

This, I tell my wife telepathically, making a thin line out

of my lips and flicking my eyebrows upwards to compound a point that needs no vocalizing, is where monosyllabic teenagers come into their own.

—So, I say cheerily over my menu as a glass shatters somewhere. —What are you going to order, guys?

I regard them all sitting there in the next booth—because somehow in the intervening years, my wife and I appear to have become the embarrassing ones that none of them wants to sit beside—each barely tolerating the other in such close proximity solely for the prospect of food and no dishes to wash up afterward.

—Chicken wings, chirrups the girl. —No wait, a burger, no wait, chicken wings.

—How big is thirty ounces? asks the youngest teen.

—Why don't you all have something from the children's menu, my wife tells him.

The three boys, sitting in sequence of age and looking like the evolution of hair, simultaneously flip their menus over then look back at my wife with pitying expressions.

—In fairness, I tell her as my wine glass rings to the nearby screeches of what sounds like a chimpanzee having its nails extracted with pliers, —it's been a while since we got away with a few rounds of chicken nuggets and spaghetti hoops.

Quite a while, as it happens, but not nearly long enough to shake the horror of the veritable slurry pit that can be made of a humble twelve-foot-square section of local eatery by the hurricane force of a single toddler intent on destruction through the medium of food, paper napkins, and a torrent of corrosive saliva.

Why restaurants persist in providing foods with bright red sauces on children's menu, is beyond me. You might just as well hand them a machinegun loaded with paintballs.

In fact, it's still enough to summon an involuntary shudder as I sit thinking of some of the messes we've left behind in our day, which, despite our best efforts, probably looked rather like the way you might picture the triage station after an explosion at a baby food factory. And although somehow—for the life of me I cannot fathom why—with each ensuing tot, we were never quite entirely put off the experience of eating out, I'm pretty sure we must at some point have considered the idea of wearing rubber butchers' aprons and surgical caps.

Truth be told, many is the meal after which my wife and I, having attempted for an hour to spoon-feed tomato sauce into a geyser and looking as though someone had sliced opened a carotid artery at our table, would hastily scrape together the hideous mountain of dissolved food, tissues and shattered crayons into a neat heap before leaving an extravagant tip and trying to flee, wailing infant under one arm still trailing the filthy, dripping high chair by one buckle.

—Order off the adult menu, I croak, shaking off the nightmare and happy to be back in the present.

In no time, the waiter is trundling off industriously to the kitchen with our two-page, mortgage-defaulting list of food items, at which point we suddenly notice how quiet it has become and I suspect my wife is thinking the exact same thing that I am.

Back in the day, the best outcome we could hope for was that the youngest would fall asleep into their food— something that happened with a disquieting frequency that bordered on narcolepsy with our second born—and occasionally we would simply hear a sort of splat, then retrieve his head out of the fluorescent mash and leave his head safely lolling off the tray as we laid into the wine.

As it happens, our neighboring diners seem to have beat a retreat with their diminutive despot and now a cleaning crew are roping off the slaughterhouse crime scene with yellow cones on which appear to be printed little icons of stick men slipping on messily masticated curly fries.

Our children tuck in, disconcertingly stripping the flesh off chicken bones and seeming to unhinge their jaws in order to fit whole halves of burgers in one go.

I stab a forkful of lettuce and sneak a grin to my wife as we notice a waitress counting mounds of wet change amid the debris and somewhere we hear the squeal of what could be departing car wheels.

—There, as the saying goes, I tell her —but for the grace of God, go we.

Fetch Me The Scissors

—We're only blessed, I tell my wife, or words to that effect:
—that our boys are long past the age where they have to write an essay when they get back to school, titled *What I Did This Summer.*

—They may still have to. It's the sort of thing we used to have to do in French.

—Well, in whatever language, it would be a bloody short story.

—I'm quite sure that the sun will shine again, not for just those three days.

—Maybe, but will they sleep through it all again?

Truth be told, the fact that our so-called Irish summer is back to seeming more like a warm, moist October again, rather than a postcard someone has sent to taunt us from the Algarve, is kind of a relief. It means we don't have to try and wrench the boys from the rancid teenage Velcro of their beds with the same weary clichés we've been shrieking ourselves hoarse with all week. *Get up, you're missing the whole summer* and the like.

On what will likely be talked about wistfully for years by 'normal families' as the nicest day of the year, last Sunday , it was almost two in the afternoon before one of us ventured up to the loft to where the second eldest and his younger brother lay entombed in what can only be described as a hermetically sealed pet cage.

The only thing missing, one couldn't help but think while shuffling, nostrils clenched, through the gloom of unbearable heat, a cross between a sauna and a rugby team's laundry bin, were wood shavings on the floor, which there may well have been, judging by the wince-inducing crunch of detritus underfoot.

And there they groggily lay, sweaty fringes plastered to their foreheads, squinting like hairy, bad tempered moles as the opening of a Velux window made an audible 'psshhhht' noise like air rushing into the hatch of a submarine after thirty days at the bottom of the sea.

—Don't even tell that story, says my wife now, —like *you* are the one who went up there."

—I'm cursed with a vivid imagination. Anyway, my stomach isn't strong enough. My breakfast wouldn't last ten seconds in the hot mushroom fog of that crypt.

Only the girl ended up tottering to the beach with us, and that was under duress.

—What ever happened to a nice family day at the seaside? rues my wife as we sit reminiscing.

—Netflix.

We were home, pink and stinging from Irish overexposure, by the time the first teenager lumbered in to the kitchen.

—We're out of cereal, was all he could mumble.

—It's four o'clock, my wife told him. —Put some shorts on. We're having a barbecue.

—I don't have any shorts, he griped. —None of us do.

—Then put trousers on and fetch me the scissors. Ever heard of cut-offs?

—I'll find some shorts, he muttered.

—We don't have a barbecue, offered the eldest sullenly. —It dissolved. In the garden. A year ago.

—We're borrowing one, said my wife. —And. We. Are. Having. A Barbecue.

The last word was said through gritted teeth.

We ended up pootling up to our allotment and ferrying firelighters and burgers to a tiny, unplanted corner of our modest patch of struggling plants, then squatting in the smoke for an hour. It was the first summer outing we'd been on as a family in what seemed like years. We looked like a troupe of new-age travelers on the hundredth day of some sort of eco-protest. It's a miracle someone didn't show up with a court order to vacate the vegetable patch.

—But, you know what? I ask my wife as we sit now behind wet windows, talking about this as if years have passed, not just three days. —It was actually quite nice to have them all together like that.

—Amazing how the three boys still managed to sit on that tiny blanket without actually looking at each other.

—Quite the feat. We may have to get consecutively smaller picnic rugs each year, just as a joke.

—Don't you remember what happened next, though?

—We all lived happily after?

—No. Well, yes. But before you drank all the wine.

—Um.

But I remember, alright the eldest upped and left on

his skateboard and didn't come home until two in the morning; the second eldest hooked his head up to some manner of handheld device and stumbled off to meet friends down the town; and the youngest teen shuffled home after much pleading.

—And our little girl got a ride home with some friends of ours.

—Who had come with more wine. I blurt this out enthusiastically, as if remembering a dream I've had.

—Then she bolted all the doors and tortured her brother for an hour from an upstairs window before letting him in.

—And it was the. Best. Summer. Ever. I slap the table.

—Well, it looks like the sun is coming out again, so you best get some shorts on this time.

—I don't have any shorts.

—Then fetch me the scissors.

—I'll find some shorts.

Steaming Open The School Report

—So, let me get this straight.

I'm perched squinting at rows of columns, numbers and ticks on our little girl's school report.

—A number one is the worst and five is the best.

—Well, says my wife. —They don't use words like 'best' and 'worst' anymore.

—Clearly, I mutter.

It looks like a spreadsheet of laboratory results, quite different from the olden-day report cards in mean little brown envelopes that we were sent home home clutching teary-eyed with fear. It was the longest walk of the year. A day of dread. Phrases like, *wait until your father gets home*, and the prospect of no money for comic books for weeks.

But the girl skipped in from school with her bright little yellow folded sheet, barely able to contain herself, beaming as we opened it, then tottered off singing.

—This is an entire pamphlet.

I'm folding and unfolding it and noticing that all of the little ticks are in the column marked 'five' or 'four'. Which is apparently a good thing. Very good in fact. Far from the reports I remember steaming open with the kettle and laboriously attempting to change Es into Bs.

Now there are sections actually titled *Behaves Well In Playground* and *Sensitive To Others' Feelings* with four possible grades, all with jolly comic-book-font computerized ticks under the column headed 'always' and for a moment I vividly recall handing over a grim report one year to my parents across the bottom of which were scrawled the words 'YOUR SON IS A TEST OF PATIENCE' underlined three times.

—Where did we get her? I say.

—Haven't a clue, deadpans my wife.

—You do realise, all that's missing on this thing are little pictures of flowers and butterflies?

—It's quite detailed actually. You have to read between the lines. Look at the comments.

The comments section is neatly printed by computer.

When I was our daughter's age, the best I could hope for was that the teacher's handwriting might be so awful, that words like 'inexcusable' or 'infuriating' under the column marked 'behaviour' would be indecipherable.

It's actually how I first began using a dictionary: desperately trying to find similar-sounding, more positive words. *I'm pretty sure that says 'inspirational'*, I'd try and tell my mother as she chased me around the kitchen table swatting me on the backs of bare legs with the envelope.

—It says here she has 'great ability for recalling information and explaining her skills to others'.

We blink at each other.

—In other words, it's hard to shut her up sometimes?

—Could be worse, says my wife.

I know what she means. Our friends' report for their five-year-old said 'loves to give the class extremely detailed accounts of what's been happening at home every day'.

—The horror.

I blanch a little at the thought and skip ahead through the comments to make sure it says nothing like that here. As I do this, I make a few idle pen marks in red.

—What are you doing? pipes the girl, suddenly reappearing.

—Correcting your teacher's punctuation.

She giggles.

In truth, this happy little school report with its schmaltzy illustration of smiling schoolchildren holding hands on the front is a blast of fresh air—the end-of-year updates on how things have been ticking over deep beneath the shaggy fringes of her secondary school brothers have not been entirely as rosy. *Smm-herrup apport-curd*, the youngest boy had murmured as he dropped an envelope on the table then promptly disappeared to a computer to resume slaughtering zombies. And when the older brother trundled in, he simply heaved a giant, heartrending sigh handed his report over, then trudged upstairs to his bedroom and slammed the door.

The murmurer's report was not all gloom, as it happens. Far beyond expectation, actually: including something about him being 'a good communicator'.

—Perhaps they've got the wrong child, I said.

—Maybe they have an interpreter, explained my wife.

The door slammer's report was a doomsday almanac forecasting a final two years of anxiety and hardship. Grinds were recommended, meaning long months of cheap meals for us and the finest wines known to man, no doubt, for the legion of grinds teachers soon to be raking in heaps of our hard-earned cash.

—Look on the bright side, I tell the boy when he reemerges.

—What? he says.

—Um…

He lumbers off again.

Still, all that hell did pay off with the eldest of the lot, who phones a little later from college where he's been finding out his own exam results.

—I got a First.

—That's good, right? I ask my wife.

—You're joking, she says. —It's brilliant.

—Well, it's clear who he takes after.

I wriggle my eyebrows. She gives me a stumped look.

—I went to college, I say defensively. —For a while.

—Lounging around on the cricket pitch outside the bar in my college with a pint in your hand while I was finishing my degree, hardly counts.

—Look at me now.

—I rest my case.

Bruce Springsteen Blaring From My Crotch

—Um, manages the bewildered hairstyle suddenly trudging into the kitchen on what could almost be stilts with flapping socks. —Can anyone tell me why all my clothes are in the rubbish?

It's the middle teen.

—Evidently, I tell him, raising my eyebrows over the rim of my coffee cup, —you missed the announcement.

—What announcement?

—The one where your *mother* told everyone that unless their clothes are in the laundry basket, not flung around the bathroom, they all go straight in the bin.

—And another thing, says my wife, suddenly appearing and startling both of us. —This house no longer offers belt extraction or pocket-checking services. If it's in the laundry basket, it goes in the wash, mobile phone and all. If it's in a heap on the floor, or on top of the basket, the whole lot goes in the bin. You have been warned.

My heart goes out to the deeply sighing teenager now hunched over the trash, morosely disentangling a scrunched up pair of trousers from an empty milk carton and several crisp bags, but she has a point.

Bad enough the family bathroom has, over the course of the summer, come to resemble an explosion in an undergarment factory, but when the deafening spin cycle of clanking pocket contents finally finishes to also reveal the dripping hulk of what was once a mobile phone, it's the parents who are suddenly the bad guys.

—Honestly, I've had enough, says my wife, as the boy shuffles off mumbling.

The hall stand is a grim testament to precisely what has her so exasperated: a cemetery of dead handheld devices. It amazes me how they can send a camera deep into the ocean to film the Titanic, or all the way out of earth's atmosphere to photograph the reaches of space, but they have yet to come up with a bloody mobile phone capable of withstanding a forty-minute cotton wash.

—I'm no longer responsible for what goes into that machine, she says. —And I'm not replacing any more phones. If they can't look after their own things, they can do without.

If only it were that easy. Unfortunately, we text more than we talk to all three teens since summer started. It's the only way to get them home for dinner or before dawn. Perhaps I can pay for replacement phones with some of the coins we fish out by the handful from the jammed dryer drum with the wreckage of keypads and circuit boards.

—You've seen the latest casualty then.

—Don't even tell me, she says from behind her hands.

It's an iPod Touch, with a shattered face. Another great Twenty First Century irony: that we are capable today of encapsulating the sum cutting edge technology in the palm of our hand, yet choose to make that device from a sheet of glass that bursts into fragments on contact with kitchen tiles.

—I don't think it was the wash this time.

She shrugs. —Either way, not my problem.

On cue, the washing machine begins making a sound like sloshing gravel. I pat my own pockets under the table to make sure I have everything as the eldest trundles in for afternoon breakfast.

—Has anyone seen my phone?

—Over to you, I tell my wife.

Later on, I have to be at a board meeting in the youngest's school, last one of the year, and sit uncomfortably for an hour with phone jammed down front of jeans. Not wanting to be the next casualty of our new laundry regime, and applying a middle-aged man's faultless logic, I figure it's the best place to put it so as not to forget it when I undress for bed, seeing as I'll have to pry it out from a painful depression in my lower abdomen.

When the meeting ends, I stagger to my feet with one dead leg and limp over to where the teachers are talking by the door, stealthily attempting to shift the uncomfortable electronic slab in my pocket without it looking too odd.

The two young women are evidently waiting to clear the room for some sort of dance class, for which the music already seems to be playing, rather loudly as it happens and, as we exchange polite parting pleasantries, I recognize the sound of one of my favourite songs.

—I love this guitar solo.

I grin and nod my head in time to the music for a moment. They smile blankly.

159

Only when I walk outside do I realise that I have somehow triggered the music application on my phone, which is now blaring Bruce Springsteen from my crotch.

—If only the sound had been that good at the RDS last week, I tell my wife glumly when I get home and relay the details of my latest humiliation.

—You, she winces, —are an incredible idiot.

OCTOBER
NOVEMBER
DECEMBER
JANUARY
FEBRUARY
MARCH
APRIL
MAY
JUNE
JULY
AUGUST
SEPTEMBER
OCTOBER

Suddenly Useful

Terrible father that I am, I have variously cast my teenage sons in this diary as mute extras in an Addams Family film, and mumbling, monosyllabic hairstyles on stilts on the last leg of a tour before the band implodes. And I am correct, of course. These are entirely accurate representations, except perhaps that I am the only one who actually harbours any desire to be in a band. I simply cannot grow hair like theirs, nor can I fake the attitude (or learn a single song or play any kind of instrument, but we won't go there).

In short, my boys are more rock 'n' roll, without even trying, than I will ever be. But this admission doesn't make me a better person. It just makes me feel rather middle-aged, irritable and out of the loop. Which, I imagine, is generally how the average parent of any teenager feels.

I never wanted to be an 'average parent', like the ones I think I remember having: cranky and out of date. I wanted to be one of those fathers who friends of my kids would say, *wow, your dad is so cool. I wish mine was like that.*

But the next minute, they're dragging their backsides around, complaining that their laundry hasn't been done, when they've only just emerged from their beds at three in the afternoon, and suddenly it's impossible to be cool and you catch yourself, sounding like your own parents, using expressions like *what time do you call this?*

It's all rather depressing and, more often than not, you find yourself feeling as though they'd get on quite well without you haranguing them about 'every little thing'. Even when you're trying to be nice, asking them about their day or what they have planned or what their friends are up to, you're greeted with a deep sigh, a withering look from deep behind some straggly mop and, at best, an *I don't know why you keep asking me that.*

Is this it? Is this what we've become?

My wife and I miserably survey the latest debris from our adolescents' nocturnal activities: dishes on the floor, trails of abandoned shoes, before beginning all over again the daily routine of shouting up the stairs to try and pry them from their beds and out of the house, with all the usual clichés that our own parents once peeled off: *pick up your things; it's lunchtime, not breakfast; you're wasting the whole summer;* and *right, that's it, you're on your own, your mother and I are moving to Paris where we're going to drink wine and make love all day for the rest of our lives.*

I made up the last bit—wishful thinking, perhaps—but you get the idea.

—It's almost as though they wish we weren't here, that they think they'd be better off without us.

—You think? says my wife, implying that it's obvious.

We're irritants, nothing more, sent by an unfair god to try their patience. We're one of the main reasons, it would seem, that life sucks. Because, let's face it, a life in which someone is forced to put down a gaming controller for thirty seconds and have a conversation, is no life at all.

And then, out of the blue, comes some petty, run of the mill circumstance that reminds you how vulnerable these gruff, towering test tubes of bubbling hormones can still actually be, and what being a parent is sometimes about, and then you experience that rare, warm flood of feeling almost useful for a change.

Right on cue, the eldest suddenly reveals that he's going to Scotland with friends.

—You're *what?* My wife and I say this at the same time

—I've been telling you about this for ages.

We look at him blankly.

—I'm being picked up for the airport at three in the morning, and I have no socks.

—Is he going with his college friends? I ask my wife as he sighs off somewhere to begin banging cupboards.

—It's Venture Scouts, he says from the other room and for a second I feel horrible that I didn't even know he still did such a thing.

I dig through my drawer and find a few bundles of hiking socks.

—Do you need boots?

I drag mine from under my bed as he stands in the doorframe scrolling through a list on his phone.

—They might be a bit big, he says quietly.

—Wear two pairs of socks. What about waterproof trousers? Do you have a jacket?

We find the things he needs, then I ask if he'd like to go to the supermarket with me, which he does, and we stroll around the aisles together, but all he really wants are a few energy bars and some mints.

—Thanks, he says when I go to pay.

I try to stay up with him until three to see him off, but I fall asleep in my clothes and when I wake up he's already gone. When I go upstairs to check, it's strange to see the sunlight pouring in to his empty room through open curtains so early.

—Did he have everything? asks my wife.

—I guess so, I say.

Even my big boots, I think glumly. Boots which, it seems, he's quite big enough to suddenly fill.

Not Birds, Bats

Uh, hub miffa derr? says the youngest teen from where he's poised over the cutlery drawer.

I look at him from where I'm cooking, then over at his sister who's wandering around, humming something tuneless at whatever invisible fluttering creatures inhabit the parallel dimension of her eleven-year-old world.

What I need is a translator.

—Does anyone speak 'teen'?

I announce this to the room.

—Subtitles? Anyone?

He uses both hands to part his curtain of his hair and in a tone that implies that I am the idiot, says:

—How. Many. For. Dinner?

—Six.

I don't mean to sound irritable, but that's how many I've cooked for since forever, even though lately it seems like we have occasionally morphed into a family of four.

—Four humans.

I try to recover a sense of humour.

—And two vampires.

The little girl stops humming and looks at me sideways for a second, then resumes her part in dinner preparations: she leans over a stool and kicks her legs in the air.

While not quite the stuff of *The Twilight Saga*, our two eldest have largely become creatures of the night this summer, usually rising well after the sun has reached its zenith, then flitting away through a hole in the hedge in the front garden, pale and thin, all dark skinny jeans, only to return well after dark.

—I'll text them, says my wife, striding in and squinting into her mobile phone, though she'd have more chance contacting them with a Ouija board.

—Be sure to only ask questions that can be answered with 'yes' or 'no'.

Her phone erupts a few seconds later. She reads the message to me. —In town with friends. Won't make it.

I'm dishing up when the text comes in from the second eldest. —Save me some.

I shrug. Usual story then. We'll leave a plate of leftovers under tinfoil and sometime between midnight and four in the morning, we'll hear a lot of flapping around and the plate will be reduced to a few bones.

—We could rent out their rooms. Just tell any tenants that we're haunted.

—Funny, says my wife.

Next day, she tries to raise the two from their lairs early, whipping open curtains in the eldest's cave, which prompts a beleaguered moan beneath the catacomb of covers. She fares little better with the other one in the loft.

Outside, what's tipped to be the hottest day of the year struggles out of a muggy morning mist.

—Can we go to the cinema? asks the girl.

—Yeah, murmurs her fourteen-year-old brother. —Less go siminna 'n' seeya fum.

—I think there's about as much chance of that today, I tell them, —as…

—Okay, fine, says their mother, clearly exasperated from the ritual of raising the dead. —Let's go see a movie.

It turns out to be a surprisingly affordable upside to our suddenly being a family of four.

—Two adults, two children, says my wife, relishing the words, and the modest total on the receipt.

—Quick, I say. —Book us on one of those family holidays that we've had too many kids to go on for the past fifteen years. I'll call us a taxi.

—You know, I'm not sure they would even miss us, she says, referring to the two back home. We chuckle then exchange looks and feel a little bad.

—Can we get popcorn? asks the little girl.

—No way, I say.

—That, explains their mother, as we step into the booming darkness just as our movie is starting, —would defeat the entire cost savings we have just achieved.

—You'll just have to wait for popcorn, I tell her, —until we're a family of three.

After the film, we wander around the shopping centre for a while, parading our two under-fifteens behind us, which makes us feel like young parents.

—We could be five years younger, says my wife.

—Wow, I say, trying to sound enthusiastic, but really I'm disappointed. Five years? Is that all? I was thinking that having just two kids somehow put us in our thirties.

—Yeah, sure, she tells me when I say this, —if we'd started having them in our teens.

—Didn't we? I pout.

Back home, it's dinner for four again, which we have outside in the sun to try and assuage our summer cinema sense of guilt. We tuck into chicken wings but, as usual, there are two little heaps under tinfoil somewhere inside.

—Look, says the little girl, suddenly excited and pointing at a baby bird fluttering around on the ground.

—*Sum miffer 'um*, burbles the full mouth under her brother's fringe. He points a boney finger at what turns out to be another baby bird.

—They're all leaving the nest, my wife says, whimsical.

—Seems they're not quite ready. Look.

On cue, a pair of bigger birds begin using their beaks to stuff food into the now gawky, squawking balls of fur.

—You know, I don't do metaphors, I tell my wife, —but if I did…

—They'd probably be cringiest metaphors ever?

—No. I pretend to be hurt for a second. —They wouldn't be birds, they'd be bats.

It's The Burglars I Feel Sorry For

It's still what seems like ages before we're supposed to go away on what could be, I think to myself, a little glum, our last holiday as a family, but the debacle of our preparations are already in high gear.

It's probably our last holiday as a family because, after this year, the prospect of the eldest being trapped in such close proximity to his siblings for more time than it takes to hoover up a meal, will no doubt be met with silence and a suitably withering look.

For now, the chaotic process of getting the house ready for our departure continues, room by room, which is a bit like tidying up after an earthquake, except without actually removing any debris, just dusting it all off and stacking it a little better.

—I would like everything in the downstairs study taken out into the garden, wiped down and put back only after the windows are cleaned and the whole lot is vacuumed.

The youngest boy picks up the lid of a pen off the floor, lumbers around in a circle examining it through straggly hair then puts it down on a pile of old school books.

—Why do we have to clean if we're not even going to be here? asks the girl, idly prying an old pair of maracas from a pile of music magazines where it's being held in place by a cobweb.

—So that when the burglars break in, I tell her, —they won't be so disgusted at the way we live.

In fact, friends of ours are staying to look after the dog while we're gone and the big clean-up is really for them, since my wife is horrified by the idea that someone should be in the house long enough to see some of the clutter that we usually hurry visitors past.

—It's like a house swap, except we don't get to be in their lovely house but they get to experience abject squalor.

—What's abject squalor?

The boys shift the sofa and reveal dead woodlice.

My wife, meanwhile, is upstairs with the phone on loudspeaker, which has been blaring holding music courtesy of the car rental company for the past half hour. It abruptly switches to a dial tone. She wails.

—Nooooooo!

—What's up? I go to see.

—I thought they'd booked a seven-seater for when we arrive, but now're telling me it's 'unconfirmed'.

—What does 'unconfirmed' mean?

—It means there was never one to start with. And now they're saying there isn't a seven-seater to be had in the whole of France.

—Can't we all squeeze into a five seater?

—No, because if we did, one of the boys would have

to be in the front because of their long legs and I'd be the one squished into the back for two hours at a time, and because it's illegal.

—Anything I can do?

—You can kill me now.

The loudspeaker goes to holding music again.

—Well, that would probably solve the problem of the five-seater.

She glares at me.

By the time I go downstairs again, we've been promised two small cars instead. We will now have to drive in convoy through France. With circus stickers on the sides, and a bullhorn blaring carnival music, no doubt.

The boys are putting the last of the unsorted papers and broken guitars back in to the study which, while brighter now and smelling like vinegar from the window cleaner, is still essentially the same wreck it was half an hour ago.

On cue, the dog lumbers in, looks around miserably for a moment and gives a vigorous shake, emitting a vast plume of dog hairs that float everywhere before settling.

—Nice when everyone helps, isn't it?

I say this to no one in particular.

—Can I go now? mutters the second eldest.

—There's more rooms in the house you know.

But he's already gone.

It's then that I realise we will probably not be able to hide the fact that being a family of six is a rather untidy business. Hopefully, our dog-sitters will understand.

—It's the burglars I feel sorry for, I tell my wife later as I root through a pile of old band tour T-shirts with which to embarrass my family while we're abroad.

—What do you mean? she says.

—Well, anyone dumb enough to go to the trouble of breaking in here, will barely have time to register their disappointment and revulsion at how people can live like this, before the poor hysterical wretch has to be rescued from our insane mutt.

We survey the study.

—You're welcome to dig in and do something about it, says my wife. —Most of this rubbish is yours.

—Actually, I tell her, retrieving a heap of yellowing newspapers from the bin and putting them back under the desk. —I kind of like it exactly the way it is.

Computer Printer Yoga

—Oh, is all I can manage as I barge in to the spare room where our computer is to find my wife in what I think is some sort of yoga position, cream all over her face and peering into the printer like it's a letterbox in a door behind which some tense drama is taking place that she's having difficulty following.

—Bloody hell, is what she says as the machine makes a sort of grinding sound and stops, then all the lights begin blinking at once.

—What are you doing? I ask.

—What does it look like I'm doing? she says, stabbing a button with her finger.

—It looks like you're trying to climb inside the printer.

—I'm trying to print out the route we're supposed to be driving on our holiday, she says between gritted teeth as something suddenly shudders to life again, sucks a piece of paper in and instantly chews it to bits.

—Well, are you going to be long? Because I'd rather like to hop in and empty the photos off my phone.

She stands up so suddenly that I flinch.

—I have booked every ticket, she says as I back away a little; —I have reserved every guesthouse, spent hours on hold to the hire company to get two cars to stuff our family into and I have planned our entire route, meticulously, and in FRENCH, and you want to 'hop in' and play around on your phone.

—Well, I croak, —if you put it like that.

—Just tell me you've packed, she says, flipping open the printer and ripping out a chunk of debris with her fingernails in a way that makes me cover up like a goalie about to receive a penalty kick.

—Almost, I lie.

—What exactly are you trying to do? asks the eldest, suddenly appearing.

—Not you as well, sighs my wife.

—Can I download something, I ask him, —while the printer is, eh, doing its thing?

—The computer is capable of doing two things simultaneously, he informs me dryly.

—It's obviously not male then, says my wife from the side of her mouth.

—Ouch, says the eldest.

—She's trying to print our route, I explain helpfully, —only the printer isn't cooperating.

—You mean this? he says, producing his smartphone like a magician doing a trick and with a flick of a finger revealing what appears to be an entire route map of our holiday, indexed by consecutive destination.

—Wow, says my wife. —Bagsy him in my car.

—He's already bagsied, I tell her.

—Liar, she says. —Flip you for him.

—No way, I say. —Rainman stays with me.

—Eh, sorry? he says.

—I gave birth to him!

We both look at her.

—I think she has you on that one, he says.

I go to our bedroom to pack and notice, with some degree of irritation, that my wife's cases are ready.

I heave a sigh, toss open my empty suitcase and blink at it. Honestly, women and packing. They spend hours making little piles on the bed, packing, unpacking again, ironing little scraps of cloth and then putting it all back together again like some sort of three-dimensional puzzle made entirely of bras and shoes.

I turn, open the wardrobe door and grab a wad of boxer shorts and band tour T-shirts and throw them into the case. Precision strike. I toss a couple pairs of combat shorts on top for good measure, then I stuff a pair of flip-flops into the side pocket before zipping up the lot.

—Bada-bing, I say and head downstairs for a beer.

—Please, says my wife, as I rummage in the fridge, —tell me you haven't just thrown a few old T-shirts into your suitcase and now consider it packed.

—Honestly, I don't know what you're talking about.

—Do I need to check?

—I will not stand here and be treated like a child.

—Remember the boxer short debacle?

—Nope.

—When you forgot to pack any and insisted on going the whole holiday Comanche style?

—Commando, I mutter. It's called going Commando.

—I don't think we can ever visit County Clare again.

—That was not my fault. I was just relaxing, feet up, and a gust of wind blew the leg of my shorts open.

—Well, I for one will forever be haunted by the look on that child's face.

—Children always look surprised. It's their default expression. Anyway, I apologised.

—Or the look on the face of the child's mother.

—And I will not keep apologising.

—Rubbish. She lobs a dishcloth at me. —You thought the whole thing was hilarious.

—One needs to have a certain sense of humour about these things.

The youngest teen lopes in and peers at his mother from behind hair. —Whub-imma tuxo mmm morum? he asks with barely a flicker of his lips.

—It's not a taxi, my wife explains patiently. —A friend is driving us all to the airport, and it's at nine.

—How on earth did you... I start to say as the boy lumbers off. —You realise that when he gets to passport control, they'll think he's standing wrong way around. All that hair, you never know which end you're talking to.

—Passports!

She shoots off in a panic.

—See? I yell after her. —I think of everything.

I swish the last swallow of beer around the bottom of my bottle.

—Honestly. This family would grind to a complete standstill without me.

You Can't Sit There

—Um, says the girl just as I've finally wrestled a cramped hand from my wheelie bag and plonked myself down in what seems to be the only free seat available to wait for our departure gate to be announced. —You can't sit there.

—I think you'll find that I very much can.

I turn the first page of my holiday book and wriggle my back side into the seat a little to emphasise the point.

—Eh. The eldest chimes in now. —No. You really can't.

This is when I realise that the entire family is looking at me with a mixture of wide-eyed trepidation and bemusement, as if I'm about to back slowly into a lamppost (which has, in fact, happened before).

—Okay, what?

I close the book and put it down with a punctuative thud to show just how much this could begin to irritate.

We're packed into a row of seats in the airport waiting

area and mine, the last available, is remarkably comfy.

I surrender with a sigh and slowly get up to look around for the half-eaten jam doughnut that someone has probably left, which has doubtless exploded under my big bottom. Only then do I notice how my seat, which is without jam, is made of luxuriously padded blue leather while everyone else's is hard plastic.

—Reduced Mobility Seating, I read aloud and my whole body gives a small but noticeable jolt at which the youngest teen sniggers. —So?

I turn back around, fold my arms and stay put.

—I am precisely what it says. In fact, I am so reduced in mobility that I am not moving at all.

—We're not sitting anywhere near you if you insist on staying there, cautions my wife.

—Look, I explain. —If a person of less mobility than me comes along, I will happily offer them this extremely comfy chair. Until then, it's mine.

—You're not supposed to offer it, chimes in the second eldest. —It's supposed to be already available.

—I promise I'll keep an eye out and spring up long before they get here.

—You really are horrible, mutters my wife from where she's now hiding behind a book.

—How am I horrible? I say, looking from teen to teen with mock indignation.

—Let me count the ways, mutters the eldest from behind a hand, as if he's trying to hide too.

—I've seen him use the disabled toilets as well, adds the second eldest and I glare at the traitor.

—Really, says my wife.

—They're cleaner, I plead, holding out my hands and

shrugging. —And you can't say 'disabled'.

—What if you came waltzing out with your newspaper under your arm to find someone waiting there who really needed it? challenges my wife.

—First off, I don't waltz. And second, I would apologise profusely and tell them that it was an emergency.

—So you would lie.

—Why on earth would I be using a public toilet at all, if it wasn't an emergency?

—Why indeed.

The eldest is staring at the ceiling as he says this.

—Right. I'm going to get a takeaway coffee. Keep my seat for me.

I spend most of the time in the queue feeling like more of a monster than I think I probably should and chewing my fingers a little as a consequence. It's not like I've made a habit of sitting in special, comfy chairs for elderly and injured people, I argue; a chair which, in all fairness, did not specifically say 'reserved'. Quickly realizing, however, that I am fruitlessly clinging to the losing end of an internal argument, I'm saved from either going back and admitting I'm wrong or petulantly resuming my seat.

—Our gate has been announced, says the eldest from where they're all standing with their bags waiting.

—Well, I only hope that the seats are as comfy there.

—Seriously, says my wife. —We *will* disown you.

As it turns out, there are plenty of seats at the gate, none of them particularly comfy, and we lounge about in a loose knot for the next wait, my wife perching with her book beside an elderly man as I set my coffee down on a little table beside her and sit opposite.

I've only just started the first paragraph of my book all

over again when she reaches over without looking, picks up my coffee and slurps at it, then takes an indulgent chug.

—Nice coffee, she says.

—It was. But I finished mine ages ago. I think that one belongs to the gentleman beside you.

She chokes, blinking at me.

It takes just a second, a single, ludicrously pleasurable full second, for her to realise that I'm joking.

—Bastard, she says, but she's drowned out by the deafening announcement that it's time to board.

—Honestly, I chuckle to no one in particular. —I don't know if I'll even get around to my book this holiday. It's far too much fun torturing you lot.

A Circus-like Convoy

With a mixture of relief and disbelief, the whole family finally lumbers down the aisle of our Ryanair flight... and instantly begins arguing over who's sitting where, because, as it turns out, no one wants to sit near me.

—Suit yourselves, I mutter with no little sense of irony given that it's just a few short years since my wife and I were trying to fob our young children off on one another. —I'm going to read my book anyway.

No sooner has the plane taken off, however, than my great narcoleptic noggin immediately tips sideways and begins soaking my shoulder in drool and, before I know it, we're already rumbling down a tiny runway beside some sort of prefab in the middle of the French countryside.

And no sooner have we disembarked with our paltry carry-on luggage and cleared passport control, than the entire airport seems to have packed up and gone home, and the six of us are left on a small traffic island in the middle of an empty car park, sweltering in the late afternoon sun.

—Look, says the little girl and we all look over hopefully to where she's pointing. —Ants, she says.

We'd booked two rental cars because, we were told, there was not a vehicle in all France large enough to accommodate our freakishly abnormal family of six and, it soon emerges through the international languages of Franglais and mime, we must now divide into two taxis to travel to the nearest town where our tiny, circus-like convoy of French bubble-cars awaits.

—Numble-fimbus dimble-hubta doobus, rues the youngest teen through his dripping fringe.

—Actually, 'normal' families DO have to do this, corrects my wife.

I lie down flat on the baking cobbles and blink into the sun. —I think I'm jet-lagged.

—We've flown for just two hours, my wife tells me. —And there's only an hour's difference in the time.

—Still, I mutter defensively.

A taxi appears, trundles laboriously around a series of car park obstacles, passes us and disappears.

—Perhaps there's an auditioning process, I offer.

—Then we're doomed, says the eldest.

As it turns out, France is only open on Tuesdays, Thursdays and a few awkward hours inbetween during which it takes everyone a little while to recover from the nationally mandated post-lunch nap, but eventually another taxi snakes around the empty obstacle course and pulls up.

—Right, says my wife. —Who's going with me?

—Go, I say, waving my hand from where I'm still flat

on my back. —I'm still adjusting to the pace.

I'm left with the eldest and middle teen, the latter of which, it seems, has been struck dumb beneath his vast, bouffant pelmet and it's only when the second taxi arrives that I realise the predicament I'm in.

My C-grade school French simply hasn't prepared me to negotiate a five kilometer car journey. All I can recall is something about the pen of my aunt residing in the house of my uncle.

—Um, I mumble, slipping into the front seat.

—Bon jour, chimes in the eldest to my amazement. —Nous allons chez Hertz s'il vous plaît.

—Ah, says the woman behind the wheel as we hurtle off on the wrong side of the road. —Irlande?

—Si, I stammer. —I mean, oui.

—Coolock! she announces, referring I think to what I recall to be a vast, desolate, jungle of criminal gangs and burned-out cars somewhere on the outskirts of Dublin.

—Nnnn, I say, peeling the fingernails of one hand off the dashboard to make a see-saw motion at her, but deciding instead, as the countryside careers past, to simply croak: — Small world.

—Coolock, she coos breathily, smiling and nodding at the magic of it all.

My wife has taken care of all the paperwork, thankfully, by the time we arrive and, in what seems like mere minutes, and just a few hours since we handed off dog and door keys to friends back home for the next two weeks, our two cars pull out slowly and terrifyingly onto a French main road.

—On the right! On the right! shrieks the eldest from behind his hands.

—I'm quite aware of what side of the road they drive on over here, I tell him, throat clicking dryly as we squeal across the meridian on two wheels, my wife in hot pursuit.

It's the start of an adventure that will, incredibly, never quite see us living down to the expectations I'd had of some sort of *National Lampoon European Vacation* movie style meltdown. In fact, we end up arguing rarely, largely due to our being divided into two cars most of the time, each driver relying on their passenger children to be combination road-sign spotters and suppliers of sticky, half-melted sweets.

—Pity your mum, I chuckle to the eldest as he switches on the sat-nav app on his phone and plonks it on the dashboard. —She's got your sister, and you know how car sick she gets.

—I'm right here, deadpans the girl from behind me, making me swerve the car slightly.

—Right, I announce. —This is how it's going to be. Spock? Set a course for our guest house on the Dordogne, warp factor seven.

—Spock? says the eldest. —Really?

—Lieutenant Uhura, I tell the girl. I need you to start handing over all the jelly babies you've got.

OCTOBER
NOVEMBER
DECEMBER
JANUARY
FEBRUARY
MARCH
APRIL
MAY
JUNE
JULY
AUGUST
SEPTEMBER
OCTOBER

A Little Warped and Strangely Ancient

I'm rifling through my bedside drawer for a pair of old cufflinks which I can't remember the last time I used, let alone why I bought them in the first place, when I come across something else entirely, something I haven't set eyes on in an age.

—Have you found them? calls my wife up the stairs.

—I'm still looking, I yell back, retrieving one from among the old coins, balled up till receipts and tangle of phone chargers from mobiles outdated a decade ago.

And there it is, at the back of the drawer, a little warped and strangely ancient, a small album containing the handful of school-era snapshots I've kept from back when the new millennium still seemed like something impossibly futuristic, and babies, cars and mortgages were far-off and outlandish ideas.

The cellophane pages crackle as I peel them apart until I come to a rather blurry, red-eyed image of me with the girl who would some day become my wife, at our school Debs, one arm slung drunkenly around her neck, each of us making a face for the camera. I'd fancied her something awful, but never actually asked her to go that night. She'd gone with someone else and, for the life of me, though it must sound terrible, I can't now remember the name of the girl I ended up bringing; someone a friend had set me up with a few days beforehand.

—Any luck? says my wife from behind me, making me jump, and I rustle around in the drawer for a minute more before seizing the second cufflink.

—Found them.

—Good. He'll be pleased.

—Glad to be of service, I say. In truth, it's just nice, in the best and most meaningful sense of that overused word, to be able to offer my eldest something he actually needs on what is still somewhat of a milestone in a young adult life, though the whole event has changed remarkably.

—I didn't even know he was going to the Debs, I tell her, tucking the little photo I've found under a book by the bed for now. He's a year late. He hadn't wanted to go the year he left school, but, it dawns on me, he'd skipped fourth year. Now he's going with his girlfriend, but this is, in fact, 'his year'.

—I don't really know that it's his kind of thing, says my wife, tidying away stray clothes down the hall as she goes, cufflinks clasped in one balled fist. —But, anyway, they're going. Be ready at six, she adds. —We're seeing them off.

As it turns out, we're picking up his girlfriend's parents and going to another friend's house for drinks and photos. This, it seems, is how it's all done now.

—And they're going in a limo, says my wife.

—Limo, I repeat, wondering at how exotic the word

seems as it rolls off my lips. A humble taxi would have been stretching it in the day of my Debs and I'm pretty sure we all sat awkwardly on the bus into town, tugging at our collars before tottering miles to a hotel function room on shoes that seemed like stiff, shiny blocks of wood.

—Does he need money? I offer, —for breakfast or whatever? I'm picturing us, almost thirty years ago, disheveled, eyelids folded into creases, squinting painfully into the garish overhead menu of McDonalds, the only thing open in the city in the early morning back then, jackets draped over our shivering dates.

—It's all included, explains my wife, —and he paid for it himself, ages ago.

—Wow, I say, meaning it.

I'm thumbing the faded photo and trying to remember why I never asked the girl in it to go with me that night, but four children and the turn of a century later, it doesn't really seem to matter much, even though the theme to *The Breakfast Club*, our anthem that night so many years ago, is now reeling through my head on an endless loop.

—Don't forget the camera, she says.

The boy and his girlfriend look nothing less than spectacular when I see them. She has dyed her hair into a rainbow and given him a matching purple fringe. He's wearing a vintage ruffled shirt with black buttons, a purple bow tie and a black suit that's sharp and slim. She's dressed in a shirt and trousers too, black with a white tie and braces and they each wear matching Converse trainers. They're not just 'cool', they're the very antithesis of the awkward teenagers in ill-fitting evening wear we were an eon ago.

—Don't they just look fabulous together, says someone as sandwiches are passed around. Cameras flash in the front yard. A car the length of a modest apartment pulls up and my son, his date and their friends laugh and cheer unselfconsciously in a knot some distance from us.

—Yes, I say, craning my neck to see. —They really do.

The gang drain their champagne, leaving empty glasses on the garden wall as they flop into their vast, luxurious carriage which glistens, all tinted windows and promise in the last of the evening sunlight.

—Changed a bit since our day, chuckles someone.

—Thank heavens, I croak and the last I see of my son before they pull away is a wave of a hand, and a fleeting flash of metal from a gleaming cufflink.

Crazy Sour

This, I think grimly, as I career through speeding traffic along the motorway, one scalded hand still smarting from the milk I boiled over earlier and a fluorescent stain from a fizzy drink that recently missed my mouth now blooming on my white shirt, *is not the way today was supposed to go.*

—And guess what? says my sole passenger, continuing a monologue from where she's perched behind me with a little bag of doughnuts on her lap. —They're tropical flavor. Tropical flavor Tic-Tacs! All different colours. Did you even know they did tropical? They must be new.

The enraged motorist from my poor lane change a minute ago is still speeding up and slowing down beside me with his window rolled down, shaking his fist and now my petrol light has begun winking, reminding me that, on top of everything else, I have forgotten my debit card.

—Ha-ha, I manage. ashen faced. —Tropical flavor, eh?

I steal a glance over my shoulder at her and the eleven-year-old beams back, impossibly beautiful in the little outfit she's chosen, oblivious to the crimson-faced man in a blue suit fishtailing along a few feet to our left, spittle now flying from his open window as he pounds the side of his car before shooting down an off-ramp.

—Have you tried Crazy Sour Skittles? she continues.

Just a few days before, we're sitting around the kitchen and she is just home from a three-day camping weekend and I can't help lamenting the fact that summer is almost over and all of our four will soon be back to the worries of school and college.

—What day is today? says the girl, finally getting a breath between tales of campfires and pony rides.

—Friday, I lie.

—Oh, she says, making a little furrow in her forehead.

—It's Monday, my wife tells her.

They both shoot me a dark look.

It feels, in fact, like we've had a month of Saturdays and I don't want it to be over. End of summer means a downhill tumble to the end of the year and, before we know it, we'll have two major state exams at our door and a little girl on the cusp of being a teenager and all the turmoil that entails. This may well be, I lament, the last summer when her foremost concerns are sweet shops and ponies.

These are the things weighing on my chest when she suddenly learns that, while away, she missed a house visit from her grown-up cousin and brand new baby.

—Oh no, she says, face falling.

And that is the second I decide that, no matter what, we'll drive to the city together, father and daughter, to visit the newborn she was so disappointed not to have seen.

—It'll be a special day.

A last warm and happy summer day before we're dusting

off school bags with kilos of books and retrieving winter anoraks from the cobwebbed recesses under the stairs.

—And we'll bring donuts, I add.

—Cool, she chirps, suddenly happy and skipping off.

—It'll be lovely, I mutter wistfully after her. —Just lovely. And somewhere in the clouds above, no doubt, the gods chuckle, rub their hands and begin conspiring.

On the morning of our daytrip, as it turns out, it's not fate or gods, just bad timing, too much coffee and a phone call out of the blue that has me all flustered, so I burn my hand on boiled-over milk then forget to put petrol in the tank, pour cola down my front and drive like a fool.

The phone call says my dad has fallen and is in hospital, so plans must be adjusted. I'll now deliver the girl to her cousins and journey on to try and make it in time for visiting hours. But from the first hint of a worried look on the girl's face, I'm determined that whatever happens, she'll have her sunny summer day out.

—Donuts, is all I say as we pull out of the driveway. —We almost forgot donuts.

—The ones with jam inside, sometimes have chocolate instead, she informs me, tanned and skinny, from behind her enormous seatbelt.

—Chocolate it is, I say, tossing the last bit of my Coke all over my front and stifling a curse as we take off. But when we stop at the shops, there are only a few grim, hard sugary things on display. —Damn, I say, rifling through the shelves irritably, not wanting to disappoint.

—That's alright, these ones are okay, she smiles, and I wonder with a twinge just who is jollying along who.

One angry driver and a reserve tank of petrol later, she's cooing over the little baby that she so badly wanted to see and, within the hour, I've managed to make it to the hospital and cheer the patient there with tales of the outlandishly awful idiot I so often am.

When I return for her, the girl is shining.

—Did you have your donuts? I say, buckling her in.

—We baked cookies, she beams.

We coast home, just making it on petrol fumes.

—So, did you have a good day? I ask as we finally tumble in the front door.

—I had a great day. Would you like a cookie?

—No, I tell her, flopping down on a stool and looking at her. —I would LOVE a cookie.

Five-Minute Tornado

It's the very last few days of the summer holidays before the school routine begins anew and the already-darkening days signal an imminent return to our morning chaos.

This mostly means heaving two of three teens out of bed and into uniforms, guiding a pre-teen girl through four full costume changes before a last minute dash down the road and, through it all, ensuring a howling dog doesn't escape to attack the postman. At least, this is how I think I remember what constitutes our household routine from two months and one full summer ago.

—Are you ready for this? I ask the dog, who gazes back from her basket without bothering to lift her head.

I'm not sure anyone is quite ready, except perhaps my wife, who has been busy organizing her way through new shoes, school clothes and book lists for weeks, without, it has to be said, much assistance from anyone.

Only our college-age eldest will remain immune from

the 8am hurricane that's to hit our house leaving heaps of clothes, empty cereal bowls and the inevitable misplaced locker keys and journals in its wake.

It's like the opening scene from *Home Alone*, except the only one left behind when the front door finally shudders is a stay-at-home dad and a nineteen-year-old in a self-induced coma who's unlikely to be parted from his duvet until after lunch, at least for the duration of September.

—We can do this, I tell the dog who rolls a single eye at me as if to say, who's this 'we'?

It's gone 8.30am when I blink my way out of a deep sleep to see what I think is my wife standing in the bedroom in a towel saying, —What time is sixth year orientation meeting this morning?

—Agggh! is what we hear next from somewhere in the loft where the boys have festered through summer. This is followed by a noise like someone falling down the stairs.

—What? is all I can manage.

—Your uniform is at the top of the stairs, yells my wife, dressing quickly now.

—Found it, he baritones dryly from somewhere downstairs, then: —Where are my shoes? Agggh!

—They're there too.

More thumps.

—Everyone try to remain calm, I croak, but my wife is already backing the car out of the drive as our front door rattles on its hinges and a teen trots out after her in socks with shoes in hands.

—That, I think to myself, squinting at the clock, —has got to be a record.

The middle boy only has to go in for an hour and his siblings are still snoring. Tomorrow he has a day off again before school begins for real. Today is like a practice run for parents: a quick breaking-in period.

The fourteen-year-old doesn't have to be in for the third year orientation until after eleven but has been preparing himself for the cold-water immersion of rising before noon by going to bed a little earlier each night: two in the morning, then one in the morning, then midnight...

—Genius, I tell him when he unveils this plan.

The girl will return to school for what's to be her final year of primary later in the week—no practice run. We've spent all of summer trying to extricate her from behind the Netflix remote and get her out to play in the fresh air, and only now, with just a few days to go before the end of the school holidays, does she suddenly decide to make friends with the little girl from up the road. It's as if these few final days of the break are a last attempt to make the best of otherwise misspent months.

—Where do you go together? I asked, the day before this morning's five-minute tornado.

—Her house.

—What do you do there?

—Watch Netflix.

—Ah.

The car rumbles back into the drive as my wife returns from the first of what will inevitably be many last-minute, panicky dashes to the school gate.

—Only four minutes late, she pants.

—Poor guy, I say. —He didn't get any breakfast. And I tell myself that the very least I'll do every evening is lay out cereal bowls and check that there's milk. —It really is all over, isn't it?

—What?

—Summer.

—Look on the bright side. She produces a paper bag which I find myself hoping might contain pastries, but she extracts a book. —The very last homework journal in the shop.

—Hey. That calls for a high five.

She slaps my hand.

The middle boy tumbles in the door a while later.

—You're not wearing your new school uniform, says my wife. We look him up and down.

—I just grabbed the first thing I found, he says irritably, tugging off last year's raggedy jumper.

—Well, how did it go?

We all look down and take in the old school trousers with a hole in one knee, a good four inches two short now and his older brother's ratty shoes.

—How do you think it went, he says, and stomps off.

My wife looks at me. —And so it begins.

Keep Your Damn Change

My brother is visiting from America where he's the bass player in a metal band. When he trudges out of Arrivals he has a shaved head and a goatee sprouting from somewhere below his lower lip. His T-shirt says 'Cannibal Corpse'.

—Wow, I say, clapping him on the back and hoping for a moment someone might think I'm in a band too. But no-one is really looking. —You look great.

I try to recall what I looked like when I was his age, my early thirties: cargo trousers, sailing shoes, Ralph Lauren shirts... There are mannequins in TK Maxx that look more rock 'n' roll than I did.

We walk to the car.

—How's the band doing?

—We fired our lead guitarist.

—Oh. I turn the key in the ignition and wince when The Pretenders, which I had been merrily thumping the wheel to all the way here, suddenly blares.

—Haha. Don't know what that is.

I turn it off. He simply smiles and shrugs.

When we're home, we catch up, in the kitchen. Teens file through shyly, mumbling polite hellos. The girl giggles.

—You look younger without your hair, says my wife, standing back to take a look.

—Everyone says that. He shrugs. —I'm like, you know, whatever.

—Guess what? I chirp, suddenly remembering. —I'm going to be a judge for the local Battle of the Bands.

—Man, he says. —That sucks.

I try not to let my shoulders droop. —Yeah. Right?

—Or, you know, whatever. He shrugs again.

—Hey, did I ever tell you I was in a band? I blurt out suddenly changing the subject. —I was eighteen. It was a punk band.

I trot off to dig out a photo, but when I do, I see I'm wearing a shirt and tie in it.

—Can't think where that photo is, is what I say when I shuffle back in.

—It's in the little red album, says my wife.

—Nope, I say. I checked.

I decide to take my brother out and go upstairs to change. The inside of my wardrobe looks like a rummage sale of second-hand band tour T-shirts—and nothing fits.

I rifle through raincoats in the utility room.

—Where's my denim jacket? I yell irritably.

I find it and give it a shake. A spider plops out. I try the jacket on, but it's so tight across the shoulders that I can't wear it without my arms sticking out, which makes me look like a penguin that's joined Status Quo, so I abandon it and grab a black leather sports jacket.

In the pub, I finally abandon any aspirations to looking cool when I catch sight of us in a mirror and realise I look like a plain clothes policeman meeting a contact.

—It's good you're here, I tell him, handing him a pint.

—It's good to be here, he says, meaning it.

We watch the sun set outside without talking.

We're sitting around the barbecue next day and the middle boy is munching a burger behind his hair.

—He's just formed a band with his friends, reveals my wife. —They're called 'Dil-arious'.

—It's Delirious, he mutters with a deep sigh. —And it's just an idea for a name.

He stomps off. I watch him go.

—I remember that boy when he was a baby.

—You might want to keep that little nugget to yourself, says my wife, —when you're judging them in the Battle of the Bands.

—I am? I mean, he's… they are? Oops.

—He plays drums, she tells my brother.

All our children have taken music lessons and our house is a graveyard of abandoned instruments. We've probably spent enough on these classes to hire Bob Dylan for a private performance. But I can't help being quite pleased that we're getting at least one band out of it.

—I can't stand Bob Dylan, reveals my brother.

I'm dropping the middle boy back to school after lunch the next day and The Pretenders are on again.

—Back on the Chain Gang! I shout over the music, slapping the wheel in time to the beat. —1983! Can you believe this was more than thirty years ago?

The boy keeps looking straight ahead. —Yes.

—So, I hear you guys are in the Battle of the Bands. Did you know I'm one of the judges?

He looks at me to see if I'm joking or not then goes back to looking straight ahead again.

—Oh, God, is all he says.

This being a cool dad, I say to myself as he lopes off a minute later, really is a rollercoaster ride.

When I stop at the supermarket, I notice The Clash are playing over the in-store music system.

—Wow, I gush enthusiastically to the young clerk when I go to pay. —Is supermarket music just getting cooler? Or am I just getting older?

The clerk blinks at me.

—The Clash, I explain, gesturing to where the music is coming from, then grinning and making a little drumming motion on the edge of the conveyor belt with my hands.

—Um, he says, sticking out his lower lip, shaking his head and handing me two cents. —Older?

I snatch the receipt. —Keep your damn change.

SEPTEMBER
OCTOBER

A Little Less Miley Cyrus

I've sworn myself to best behaviour as we prepare to set off with the youngest to tour a prospective secondary school for next year, an all-girls one as it happens. I've even squeezed myself into one of the last remaining shirts in my wardrobe that still has a full set of buttons, though one pops off as I tug it over the regulation band tour T-shirt. *No off jokes or inappropriate remarks*, I mutter to the mirror, giving myself what I think is a meaningful look. But when the girl skips into the kitchen I can't help teasing. —Perhaps you should wear something a little less Miley Cyrus?

Our daughter frowns. —Who? is all she says.

We file out to the car in the September gloom. I feel like I have moon boots on, it's all so surreal, the idea that this time next year I could be the father of a convent girl.

—It's not a convent anymore, corrects my wife. —There are no nuns.

—Still, I mutter. —Weird.

I catch a glimpse of our daughter in the rear view mirror. Does she look plausible as a cast member from St Trinian's? *God,* I think, shuddering. *I hope not.* And do I look like the neurotic, aging father of a girls' school student? She's only just starting sixth class in her little mixed national school and when I walk her to the gates in the morning, I'm still somehow able to fool myself that I'm way too young and cool to be a dad.

Alas, I lament to my sagging, fortysomething eyes in the little letterbox reflection as we hurtle along the road: with her three older siblings already in the throes of either state exams or college studies, I'm more a bargain-basement Ozzy to a soon-to-be Kelly Osbourne, which makes me shudder again. *Ugh. No way.* But then I look back again at the skinny little long-legged thing in the back seat in her favourite Cherub Agent T-shirt, and I can't imagine her ever possibly being anything else.

When we arrive at the prospective new secondary school, the other parents seem older than us.

—They're probably not, you know, my wife confides.

—Hmmph, I say.

I'd expected a huge crucifix above the gates but there is none. First sign of some scary statue of a bloodied, dying Christ, I promise myself, and we're history. You won't see us for the plume of dust behind our squealing wheels.

It's a far cry from the all-girls schools that loomed mysterious from behind high walls when I was a kid, and I can't help recalling that the last time I was on the grounds of such a place, I was frogmarched back to the street, suspended by one ear from a gnarled finger belonging to a scary woman in a black habit.

Being from a large, mixed comprehensive school, my teenage friends and I had been fascinated by the two local convents and the legions of uniformed girls inside. We had no idea what to do if we ever met one. All we wanted, for some reason that made perfect sense at age fourteen, was to sneak in and write our names on something, a token of bravado for the angels populating these haunted houses guarded by dark ghosts.

—I should have brought a marker, I mutter, feeling hopelessly out of place as we trundle in to the milling lobby, my skinny little girl's small hand lost in mine.

—I have a pen, says my wife. —Paper too.

We're assigned a young guide for our tour, which is the first surprise: we know her. She's the lead singer in the older middle teen's band; confident, charismatic, not the kind of student I expected to meet in this place at all.

Our little girl grins up at me, eyes sparkling and gives my hand an encouraging squeeze.

—I know, I know, I whisper down to her. —It's her. Who knew?

—Hello, beams our guide pleasantly. —Welcome to our school, which we're very proud of.

As it turns out, there are no scary statues or dusty oil paintings. The walls are festooned with bright artwork, trophies and school photos of smiling faces.

As we totter along, peering through windows into neat, modern classrooms, I try to imagine our daughter gliding through these corridors, looking all grown up and splendid and it's all I can do not to bawl.

—Amazing, I croak.

After the presentation by teachers, through which the girl yawns and snuggles, small in the seat between us, we file back out with hundreds of other parents, heads reeling with information. We have only days, we're told, to get our applications in for the following year. Days in which to decide whether the girl should go to the mixed secondary where all three of her three brothers have gone, or somewhere entirely beyond any of our experience.

—What does she think? I ask when we get home and our charge does hopscotch, humming off down the hall to plug herself in to the Disney channel.

—She's quite adamant.

Of course. It was too much. What were we thinking?

—She made up her mind before we even did the tour. Far as she's concerned, it's the girls' school.

—I think I need a lie-down, I sigh, suddenly exhausted. —Wake me up in about six years, will you?

Laughing A Little Too Hard

My wife and I decide to drop everything and drive into the city to spend some time with each other. This, we agree, is one of the good things about working for ourselves from home, to be able, very occasionally, to clear the decks and skive off, to have a day on the lam.

—It'll be another Ferris Bueller's Day Off, I tell her. —We'll hit a gallery. Have some lunch.

—Can we have one day out, she says, —without you comparing it to a movie from the 1980s?

As it turns out, dropping everything isn't quite so simple. The two younger boys, who come home for lunch from school each day, have to be catered for, entailing all the raw materials for a passable midday meal be laid out, with everything bar step by step instructions on (a) lifting fork to meet (b) mouth.

—Can't you just give us cash for the shops? says the younger of the two.

—Have you lost your mind? says my wife.

Arrangements must also be made for the girl to be picked up from her school and to go to a friend's house for the afternoon.

She stands at the door before school, bag packed as if she's off on a two-month polar expedition.

—Seriously? I say.

Eventually, however, everyone is duly briefed and despatched and we find ourselves alone together with nothing but a rather blustery Monday stretching ahead.

As we leave the house, I run one finger along our dented people-carrier with mock mischievousness.

—Dare we take the Alhambra?

—It's that or the train, says my wife through what seems to be a rising gale.

—And that wouldn't be very Ferris Bueller, I say.

—Neither is having a four-day beard and a thirty eight inch waist, she says.

—I don't know, I tell her. I think they rather suit you.

We take the minivan and I negotiate the turn onto the main road with one dead arm and hurtle off towards the city bound traffic.

—Woo-hoo! I yell as we shudder along, three feet at a time between lorries.

—I think we should turn here for the parking garage, says my wife eventually, as we crawl into the city.

—Oh, I say, —You mean down the street with the giant blue sign with a 'P' and an arrow on it?

—You're not indicating.

—I'm in a left-turn lane.

—You're in a bus lane.

—I know where I'm going, I say, promptly missing the

street with the parking garage and finding myself inching along between honking taxis again.

—This, I mutter, —happens to be a short cut.

Some considerable time later, perspiring and peering through steamed-up windows, the parking garage we were looking for suddenly emerges, surprising us both.

—See? I say as we descend the ramp and I pluck a ticket out of the machine.

—Better give that to me, she says as we squeal through the underground warren and finally find a space.

—I think I'm quite capable of safely retaining a parking ticket, I tell her, to which she gives me a look, and I grudgingly hand it over.

—Remember the number of the space we're in.

—Easy, I tell her. —Thirty sixty: my age and yours.

—Funny guy, she says.

The art gallery we'd wanted to visit is closed, so we wander down through the crowded streets stopping at clothes shop after clothes shop.

—Why do I get the feeling that this was the plan all along? I say to my passing reflection.

In a shoe shop, I pick up a Doc Martin boot. —I probably couldn't get away with it anymore, I say, thinking, in fact, that I probably could.

—Probably not, says my wife.

I run a finger over the considerable price tag.

—You're probably right, I say, and I put it back.

In another shop, she emerges from behind a curtain in a flowery dress.

—Too short? she asks.

—Never, I say.

—For my age though, she says.
—Buy it, I tell her.
She puts it back.

We end up in Trinity College where Freshers' Week is in full swing and wander through the cacophony of marquees. It brings us back to the days when we wouldn't have thought twice about Doc Martins or short dresses, if we'd had the cash, and we lose each other several times in the melee.

Students with clipboards and costumes are accosting one another with free pizza and badges to join various clubs and societies. We walk through these as though we're utterly invisible.

My wife decides to phone the eldest, who's starting second year, proof, if any were needed, that our time of cool clothes and college bars truly harks back to an age when Matthew Broderick still had a twenty six inch waist.

The eldest, as it turns out, is somewhere right here with us in the square and we meet him minutes later under the campanile.

—Well, he smiles as we all go off together to find somewhere for lunch, —did you join any societies?

—Strangely, chuckles my wife, —we weren't handed so much as a flyer.

—Not even by the Mature Students' Association, I add mournfully and everyone laughs a little too hard.

Mouldering Mugs

—I have just cleaned the sink in the kids' bathroom, I announce to my wife, only realising as the words leave my mouth just how pathetic this sounds.

—Congratulations, she says.

—Well, I tell her, sensing that I'm digging a hole for myself, —it looked as if it hasn't been done in years.

She glares at me in a way that makes my hands creep front of my crotch. —Oh? she says. —Really.

—I'm only amazed, I babble, desperately trying to deflect attention back on to the hairy teenagers and their little sister who have all just stomped off to school and college after their daily rampage, leaving exploded laundry, cereal bowls and smushed-up teabags in their wake, —that they manage to get any toothpaste in their mouths at all, by the state it was in.

—And who, says my wife, emphasising the word 'who' so that I know precisely who, —do you think has been cleaning all the sinks around here, all the other times you don't manage to get around to it?

—Ooh, I say, squinting and clutching my chin, —Don't tell me. I know this one.

—Well, she says, —since you're such an expert on cleaning sinks, you can be in charge of all of them now.

—I do my bit, you know, I mumble, though the fact is, no one in our house is quite an aspiring Nanny McPhee, much as we'd love to just magic away the carpet of hair that drops off the dog every minute, or the army of crusty crumpled socks that seem recently to be multiplying in a manner that is frankly frightening. There always just seems to be something better to do.

—Have you ever, says my wife, using the word 'ever' like a finger to jab me, —cleaned a toilet in your life?

—It's on my bucket list.

—Would that be the same list, she says, —that includes the gutter out back that needs mending, or the tap behind the washing machine that needs fixing so that the laundry, which mysteriously finds its own way down the stairs twice a day without your help, doesn't come out boiled?

—I think I'll go do the dishes.

—That. Would. Be Wonderful.

I set about going room to room, gathering up mouldering mugs, starting in the loft where the youngest teen has an entire collection caked with evil microwave brownies.

If only, I rue as I clatter back down the staircase, that boy could hoover up dust the way he does useless facts.

—The human body, he once revealed at dinner, —sheds between thirty and 40,000 skin cells every hour.

—Well, I had said, —it's about time you lot started sweeping up after yourself then.

Alas, they can barely help clear up together after dinner without United Nations intervention. The nightly ritual, one of the few chores we've managed to offload, routinely ends with shrieks and slamming doors.

The Evening Chorus, my wife calls it.

—Sweet, aren't they? she'll say in the living room where we retreat as war breaks out.

—Things of beauty, I'll say as the windows rattle and the dog crawls behind a chair.

Actually, they're best left to get on with it. Try to oversee proceedings and you risk losing your sanity.

You can kid and cajole them, threaten, entice or berate, with little more result than a half-hearted, slow motion dragging of dish cloths around the room, each far more concerned about what the other is failing to do.

—Stop worrying about what someone else is or isn't doing, my wife will tell them, and just get on with it!

But the sheer effort of delegating generally ends up being so bloody exhausting, we'll let them off the hook sooner or later and either do it ourselves, or say 'to hell with it' and collapse together in front of the telly with wine.

And so it is that we make do, a little toothpaste on the sinks notwithstanding.

Fact is, I think to myself now as I lob the last dirty dish into the suds, we could spend all day scouring the house and be back to where we started in the morning. That's life in a family of six, plus one dog, and one fish that is encased in a cube of dark green jelly.

It's a messy business.

That night, we do actually end up leaving them all to their own devices as we head off to a show in the city. They're instructed to cook for themselves and clean up after.

—Do you reckon the Evening Chorus will happen without us? I ask my wife when we're safely a full train journey away from whatever chaos is or isn't happening.

—You mean like, if a tree falls in a forest and no-one hears it, does it make a sound?

—Be great if we had a 'nanny-cam' hidden in the kitchen so we could see what's going on right now.

—Seriously, says my wife. —I'd really rather not know.

Poor Ozzie

I spend half my life trying to prove what a rock'n'roll dad I am, and routinely end up succeeding in doing little more than making a complete plonker of myself.

It's put-up or shut-up time when I'm asked to help organise the town music festival and stage a large outdoor concert, and the fantasy of being a promoter swaggering around all day in a black T-shirt with a walkie-talkie crumbles, revealing a reality of panic attacks about weather and ticket sales followed by fourteen hours of running all over the place on a diet of half a Mars bar.

And it's not all about me, for a change. The girl has entered a talent show, another festival event, and reached the final singing 'Mad World' by Tears For Fears.

—Who? she says.

I show her the music video I still remember from when I wasn't much older than she is now.

—That's not the version, she says, turning away and

marching off with the other half of her duet, the two of them giggling into their fists and shaking their heads.

Meanwhile, the middle teen's first foray into the mosh pit that is the festival Battle of the Bands approaches, at which I am one of the judges, much to his shame.

The night he plays, I'm blown away. They're not the best on the bill, but they take it seriously and have a load of fun and, I realise once again, it really isn't all about me as I sit at the back of the hall in the dark, the middle-aged man with the pen and clipboard, while his friends cheer and chant his name afterwards and he pops back through the curtain and jokingly takes a bow.

—Hey, you guys were great, is what I tell him later, holding out my fist for a manly bump as he mills around with his crowd outside.

He looks at my fist, shoves his skinny arms into his pockets and spins around on his heels, so I give the air a little punch as if that's what I was going to do all along.

The night before my big concert, the girl is almost due on stage for her final as I'm helping the sound and light crew set up nearby, or at least I'd like to think that's what I'm doing. One of them hands me a spotlight and I buckle under the weight.

—Just hang it over there, he says.

I struggle with it for twenty minutes, finally standing back, coated in perspiration and grime, admiring my handiwork.

—There, I announce.

—There's eight more, he says, and I wilt.

Eventually, I have to go. —My little girl's in the talent show, I explain. —They're singing Mad World.

Oh, says the sound engineer. —Tears For Fears. Cool.

I arrive just as they're on and she's nothing less than lovely. As she resumes her seat with the other performers, I go over for a hug. —Ew, she says, recoiling then collapses in fits of giggles with her friends.

She doesn't win in the end, but joins all the contestants on stage and the way she smiles and claps her hands for the winners make me very proud.

The next day is spent running around organising. First, a smaller afternoon gig for hundreds of kids, which goes off without a hitch; then clearing the venue as six bands, totalling some thirty musicians, arrive in from everywhere with piles of gear for the main event. It's organised chaos, but the weather has held up and ticket sales seem reasonable as tens of volunteers assemble to help steward a night of music that's been months in the planning.

—Right, I say to no one in particular, —let's do this, and I gulp down the last of a can of hideous glow in the dark energy drink and am promptly stung, deep inside the throat, by a wasp.

—Ack, I croak. —Ack! Ack! Ack!

—Eh, you all right? says someone as I flail around, blood draining from my face.

Luckily, I am, eventually. My throat doesn't swell up and I don't keel over like I thought I might, but the incident haunts and sickens me for the rest of the evening and I go from choking and gagging to swallowing sore, as sound checks give way to punters and the support acts roar.

As the night wears on, I finally find myself sitting hunched in a back room, sipping anti-sting serum, as the headline act hits the stage outside and a confetti cannon showers a shrieking audience. The night is a hit, but I feel anything but the music impresario I'd hoped.

215

This is when the lead singer of one of the earlier bands, all shades and tattoos, stumbles across me.

—Man, he says, —did you really swallow a wasp?

My stomach hitches at the memory.

—Ugh.

—Dude, that's hardcore, he says, with what seems like sincere awe, and some of his band mates come over and chime in too. —Legend, says someone else.

Poor Ozzie Osbourne, I think to myself as the main act reaches a crescendo just behind the wall and the packed venue goes wild—he had to bite the entire head off a bat for some rock cred. All I needed was a wasp.

But I guess we all have to start somewhere.

1,071 Complete Changes of Outfit

It's almost a full year since I first began chronicling the fables and foibles of a flailing, forty-something father of four, and this seems as good a time as any to take stock.

That's fifty one weeks, I think to myself, ticking off our misadventures in the air like invisible fingers and looking like one of those nodding dogs on the dashboard of a car, of chaotic school mornings and misspent weekends, of perpetually exploding laundry baskets, of trying to decipher the muffled mutterings from behind teenage hairstyles and giving out to the dog for flinging itself at the front window to get at the postman; 357 days or 1,071 complete changes of outfit if you're counting from behind the slammed door of a preteen daughter. That's an awful lot of knickers flung around the floor.

—You realise I come off worst in all this, says my wife.

—I rather think it's me who comes off worst, I tell her.

—But you make it sound like I spend most of the time shouting at everyone and our house is a complete mess.

—Well...

—If this were ever published, I could sue, she says.

—In fairness, the picture I paint of myself is not exactly Dad of the Year. As if I actually spend half my life shuffling around in a dressing gown avoiding all household responsibilities, and the rest of the time wearing old band tour T-shirts, driving the car badly and harping on about old movies and 1980s music.

—Well...

—Keeping a diary is not like a Facebook profile or something, I try to explain, —where you can just take a photo of your dinner and try to fool everyone into thinking that your life is some sort of perfect, tasty little dish.

—But you do that as well, she says.

—Bad example.

She's right, of course. Family life is far more complex than any sort of snapshot, whether in words or with a cameraphone. Every day is a long and arduous process of negotiation around countless landmines.

From the first moment you pry open one crusty eyelid in the morning to the last moment of the day when you find yourself alone on the sofa with the shopping channel on having fallen asleep after too much wine (that's just you, my wife points out), it's a myriad of wins and losses, the best of times and worst of times, often all rolled up into one blurry whirlwind.

And before you know it, a whole year has gone by and you find yourself wondering, what's changed?

Well, in the average household of two financially emaciated and emotionally exhausted parents, three towering, hairy monosyllabic teens, one pretty little ticking preteen time bomb and a psychotic dog: nothing and everything.

Exactly a year ago we were riddled with angst over our eldest's eighteenth and whether we should allow him to buy alcohol for his party. Now he's facing into his twentieth year on this planet, a year in which he may well decide to go off to a college in California.

—It's called Erasmus, explains my wife, referring to the college exchange program.

—Never heard of them, I say, conforming to my own caricature. —What sort of music do they play?

The second eldest is bog snorkelling his way through the quagmire of the Leaving Certificate and, on the few occasions that he's able to come up for air, must leaf through reams of bewildering choices for Third Level based on the increasingly narrow range of subjects that he's either good enough at or enjoys.

It's simultaneously heartbreaking and terrifying and I long for the relative simplicity of one year ago when all this was still endless school terms and one full summer away.

Teen number three has gone through an entire metamorphosis, from fair-haired schoolboy with a high little voice announcing bizarre factoids at the dinner table via an entire compendium of 'Ripley's Believe It or Not' annuals committed to memory; to droll, six-foot, baritone, inextricably connected to every screen in the house by a complex system of wires and cables.

It's the Junior Cert for him now: unfortunately neither 'Ripley's Believe It or Not' nor 'Grand Theft Auto' appear to be featuring on the syllabus. But try telling him that.

The youngest is enjoying her final year in primary, between mood swings and growing extra bits – and it's becoming more difficult by the day to overlook the fact that she is fast developing into a volatile chemical cocktail that could well detonate into full-blown shrieking teen at any time.

But the dog still stands guard at the door each day, just a few infuriating inches of mahogany between her and the juicy, delicious postman; and the same fish, Moustachio, I almost killed the last time I cleaned the tank, almost six months ago, still struggles around its dimly lit cube of lime-green gel.

We're barely bruised, we six plus dog and fish, and never beaten – just a little short on socks each morning it seems and, oh, 'we never have anything to eat in this house' I've just been informed, at least I think that's what was muttered grumpily through a bushel of bed-hair; and my wife still gets them all up and out the door each day through the medium of roars.

—Seriously, she tells me, —you're to stop saying that.

—Okay, I tell her. —I promise.

About David Diebold

David Diebold is also the author of *This Is How We Dance* (Monument Media Press, 2019). He has written for *The Irish Independent, The Irish Daily Mail, The Business Post* and also for *The Herald,* where his regular weekly column of seven years was a finalist at the National Newspapers of Ireland Feature Writer of the Year award in 2011, and NewsBrand Ireland Popular Columnist of the Year in 2016. His writing has featured in *Press Gang: Tales from the Glory Days of Irish Newspapers* (New Island, 2015), and in *Spontaneity* magazine. A regular radio guest, he has been on *The Ryan Tubridy Show,* (RTE Radio 1), *The Last Word* (Today FM), and *The Tom Dunne Show* (Newstalk). A native of California, he now lives by the sea near Dublin, Ireland, with his wife, two of his four now grown-up children, and Pepper the dog.

Thanks

Diary of a Wimpy Dad made it in to your hands thanks to all those who helped with advice or practical help for more than a year since *This Is How We Dance* was launched in early 2020. They are, nearest and dearest, my wife Emily, a writer and editor in her own right; son Jonathan, a detailed proofreader; son Zachary, who designed the book's website, and Millie Baring, who designed the cover with humour, passion and skill. In the trade, Marianne Gunn O'Connor took the time to be encouraging, as did Simon Hess. Sophie Grenham and Ruth McKee are, as always, hugely supportive and inspiring, while journalists Pat Carty, Sue Leonard, Nadine O'Regan, Ken Phelan and Alan Steenson in particular made publicising through a pandemic a pleasure, as did, on radio, Daniel Cahill, Tom Dunne, Derek McCarthy, Paul McLoone, Sue Nunn, and Ryan Tubridy. Thanks also to my 'beta readers' Martin Bridgeman, Susan Hennessy, Lorcán O'Toole and Jana Vondrusova, and all those with an encouraging word.

Also out now:

This Is How We Dance

DAVID DIEBOLD

At good bookshops nationwide or direct from
www.monumentmediapress.com

Monument Media
Dublin, Ireland

About **This Is How We Dance** by David Diebold:

From struggling actor to wannabe cook, aspiring filmmaker, and national newspaper hack, David Diebold's unconventional life has placed him in some bizarre and precarious predicaments.

He has blagged his way onto the stage with the Kirov Ballet for an entire run of Le Corsaire without ever having danced; fibbed his way into a busy kitchen and cooked for Senator Ted Kennedy; and completely cocked up a job as a stripping vicar.

Strangest of all, perhaps, is the family backdrop to this rather odd journey, in which David discovered that his sister was actually his mother, and his real father, a former roadie with American hit band Three Dog Night, who he tracked down with an investigator, was a Hollywood movie special effects expert.

By turns humorous and heartbreaking, these 52 vignettes of life, love and loss are soul-searching, searingly honest, and just plain strange...

Praise for **This Is How We Dance:**

'Fifty two forways in to flash memoir ... stunning'
—Ferdia Mac Anna, AUTHOR, THE ROCKY YEARS

'A whirlwind of emotions based on life, love and loss, evoked in 52 personal stories afford a wonderful insight into the author's life. Diebold's unique style makes you happy, sad and hysterical in a short number of pages. A brilliant read.'
—Amy Finnerty, RTE CULTURE

'Happiness is here in abundance, in the small and large things: the glitter on a card made by a child; the smell of homecooked burgers; the freedom of the road. There are those relatable moments in life: watching your child grow up, and letting them go; falling in love; finding a friend. But there are also things unique to the author, a family history so unusual and complex it is worthy of a documentary—yet you never feel on the outside. The stories that explore the stranger aspects of his background feel as natural and close as those set in the supermarket on the main street of Skerries, Dublin, where Diebold lives. This is his talent—making the particular universal, and the universal particular.
—Ruth McKee, EDITOR, BOOKS IRELAND MAGAZINE

'Finely sliced and smartly spiced, a feast for friends and family. Read this and yours will seem quite normal. Fiery, finger-licking, lipsmacking good'
—Liz Ryan, AUTHOR, THE YEAR OF HER LIFE

'I envy David Diebold. That chap is one of the wittiest, sharpest and finest storytellers in the game. Just don't tell him I said that. He'll only want it in writing…'
—Chris Wasser, ARTS JOURNALIST, HERALD FILM CRITIC

'This magical book will make you laugh, look again at your own family, and pretend not to cry as David Diebold breaks your heart with his clear-eyed observation'
—Terry Prone, AUTHOR, RUNNING BEFORE DAYBREAK

'David Diebold is a gloriously funny writer, in both the 'ha ha' and 'peculiar' senses of that word'
—Olaf Tyaransen, AUTHOR, THE STORY OF O

'Quite the tale, and told with such candour'
—Ryan Tubridy, THE RYAN TUBRIDY SHOW, RTE RADIO 1

A note about the book cover's creator

Millie Baring is one of those rare specimens of human that gets shit DONE. Need an illustration? In your inbox the next day. Need some wine? She can *make* it. Need a three-part jazz harmony of your favourite pop song? She can write it. Need someone with another niche talent? She knows them. Need a therapist? She's in training. Once you've finished reading this book, you might see why we became firm friends after my wife and I accidentally spent 24 hours with her where she lives – in a castle, on an island, surrounded by wallabies – but that's a story for another day. Want some Millie in your life? www.millustrations.co.uk and www.islandclub.co